SEPHARIAL ON MONEY
---

the complete texts of

Law of Values
(pages 3-36)

Silver Key
(pages 39-122)

and the monograph,

Arcana, or Stock and Share Key
(pages 124-139)

BY

SEPHARIAL

AUTHOR OF
"COSMIC SYMBOLISM," "A MANUAL OF ASTROLOGY,"
"A MANUAL OF OCCULTISM," "THE KABALA OF NUMBERS,"
"KABALISTIC ASTROLOGY," ETC.

Astrology Classics

ISBN: 1-933303-22-0

This compilation Copyright © 2007 by William R. Roell.
All rights reserved.

Published by
Astrology Classics

The publication division of
The Astrology Center of America
207 Victory Lane, Bel Air MD 21014

On the net at www.**AstroAmerica.com**

THE
LAW OF VALUES

An Exposition of the Primary
Causes of Stock and Share
Fluctuations

BY

SEPHARIAL

Author of
"A Manual of Astrology," "A Manual of Occultism,"
"Cosmic Symbolism," "The Silver Key," etc.

CONTENTS.

	PAGE
INTRODUCTION	7
CHAP. I. GENERAL PRINCIPLES	9
II. PLANETARY VALUES	12
III. EFFECTS OF TRANSITS	14
IV. EFFECTS OF ASPECTS	20
V. SENSITIVE POINTS	24
VI. HOW TO INVEST	28
VII. HOW TO AVERAGE	30
VIII. CONSIDERATIONS	34

INTRODUCTION.

In the following pages I have given some valuable hints to those who are able to invest their money and take their dividends. They will be able, with the assistance of my book, to buy cheaply and to clear out before prices recede from the highest. It is not to be supposed that I give any of my keys, which constitute the "Arcana," and which can only be had under agreement of a binding nature, but the reader will be able to take advantage of genuine information contained in the pages of "The Law of Values," at whatsoever time he is in a position to put money in a lock-up investment. Of the actual working value of this system there can be no doubt whatsoever, for illustrations are given showing the application of the principles involved to the actual state of the markets according to official returns. With these figures there can be no cavilling, and when it is further shown that the same factors are repeatedly followed by the same effects, not in one part of the world only, but in every part whose financial interests are represented on the Stock Exchange, there can be only one conclusion, and that undoubtedly will be in favour of Astrology as the master-key to safe and profitable investment.

This is my second contribution to Astrology as a financial science, and I have been induced to write the book in the belief that the sooner we bring the science down from the clouds, where would-be Esotericists have incontinently hurried it, the sooner it will gain a proper recognition in a practical world. Later, when it is found by the man in the street to have a body and consistency, and that it can talk his own language, doubtless he will be the readier to admit that it has also a soul and can be studied from an entirely different point of view with equal benefit to the intellectual

The Law of Values

and spiritual man as it has proved useful to the material and physical man. The point need not be laboured. To those who profess Astrology I would say, feed those who are in the nursery, give them a material grip on the practical side of things, and keep your academics for the forum. What is the binomial theorem to children who can only appreciate what they can see and handle? There is an orderly process of development in thought which should be followed in all our schools, and which passes from science to philosophy, and from philosophy to ethics.

Science is what we know about a thing, philosophy what we think about that which is known, and ethic is the effect of that thought upon our conduct. Before we can profitably make an Esotericism of Astrology, we have to prove that it is a science. It is claimed for Astrology that it is the science of foreknowledge, and the man who cannot turn it to account when he has proved its scientific integrity is not worth troubling about.

I have written this book for intelligent and practical men of the world, who are, or will some day be, in a position to employ money, and I have given rules and proofs such, as will enable anybody to employ their means to the best advantage. These preliminary notes will prepare the reader for the study of the book itself.

SEPHARIAL.

CHAPTER I.
GENERAL PRINCIPLES.

The apparent cause of all fluctuations in the value of any security or commodity whatsoever, is the balance of supply and demand. The non-apparent and primary cause is the response of terrestrial nature to planetary influence. In this statement I am suggesting the operation of a cosmical law of planetary interaction, a concept that is entirely agreeable to the doctrine of the solidarity of the universe. If crops fail, whether they be wheat, cotton, coffee, or tea crops, the values of such supplies as are in sight are naturally increased, and similarly a depreciation occurs when crops are abundant. But when we come to enquire as to the failure of crops or their plenitude, we have to look further than the earth in which they were sown or the air by which they were blighted or vitalized, as the case may be. We have, in fact, to refer to planetary interaction and those cosmical laws by which the integrity of the system is maintained. The obvious law of action and reaction, which is referred to as responsible for the stability of the universe, but which in fact has been latterly referred to as the unstable equilibrium—a paradoxical phrase—is to be seen at work in the Stock and Share Market as surely as it is in the universe at large.

Let us take it as a working hypothesis that the planets act and react upon one another, producing a variety of perturbations and reactions, not only in the bodies themselves, but in the atmospheres surrounding them, and in that more tenuous and subtle medium which is called spatial ether, which is continuous of the intermolecular ether permeating the earth and all planetary bodies from centre to periphery. Then it will follow that even the brain and nervous system of man are subject to the stimulus of etheric vibration, and

The Law of Values

thus to planetary action. With this working hypothesis it will be possible to show reason for man's invariable response to the immediate action of the planets in their various geocentric relations, their conjunctions and oppositions, and their occursions to the various signs of the zodiac.

Before we can rightly estimate the effects of these interplanetary relations, however, it will be necessary to make some research, first of all to determine what countries or interests are related to the several signs of the zodiac, and next to ascertain the influence of the various planets in these signs.

We are fortunately in possession of a fair amount of traditional knowledge on both these points, sufficient to enable us to bring the matter to an empirical test.

Proceeding along these lines, we find that the twelve signs of the zodiac are related to various territories already defined and well-known to the ancients. Claudius Ptolemy, who was one of the earliest, if not, indeed, the first of geographers in Europe, delivered certain descriptive charts delineating the countries known to him and indicating the zodiacal sign to which each territory responded. The sign-rulership of various old countries has been traditionally handed down to us, and other parts of more recent development have been empirically referred to their respective signs. Thus we know that the following countries are ruled by the signs against which they are set :—

Aries: England, Denmark, Judea, Peru, Germany.
Taurus: Ireland, Persia, Italy, Chile.
Gemini: Wales, United States of America, Egypt.
Cancer: China, Holland, Africa.
Leo: France, Australia.
Virgo: Turkey, Uruguay.
Libra: Argentine Republic, Japan, Austria.
Scorpio: Morocco, Brazil.
Sagittarius: Spain.
Capricorn: India, New Zealand, Mexico
Aquarius: Russia.
Pisces: Portugal.

There are, of course, many other countries under each of these signs, some of which are under scrutiny and test,

General Principles

others of no great political or commercial importance being omitted. The above will, however, serve for the purpose of the present exposition of the Law of Values.

When, therefore, certain planets transit these signs, or form important configurations therein, or when the eclipses fall in them, the countries related to those signs undergo political changes which affect the stability of the markets they control. In a subsequent chapter this will be fully explained and dealt with in a practical manner.

CHAPTER II.
PLANETARY VALUES.

As a result of centuries of experience by successive students of planetary influence in human life, we are able to ascribe in the most positive manner certain characteristics to the various planets of the solar system. The signs of the zodiac affect nothing of themselves, and cannot be said to have any active influence in the mundane affairs. But when any sign is occupied by a planet, that body becomes a focal centre for the collection and distribution of cosmic influences. The sign occupied by it at the same time gets "coloured" or affected by the planet. The specific natures of the planets, so far as they affect the trend of market values and the stability of those securities controlled by the countries related to the signs they occupy, are briefly as follows :—

Neptune produces democratic disturbances, anarchy, chaos, confusion. It tends to schemes and plots, "rings" and rigging of the markets.

Uranus produces sudden upheavals, revolutions, strikes and insurrections. It brings about sudden fluctuations in values, and has a disturbing effect on securities.

Saturn brings famines, failure of crops, disasters of various sorts and national depression due to political reverses and general want or popular discontent. Its effect on the market is to produce a marked depression or deflation of security values.

Jupiter brings an expansion of internal resources and industries, the opening up of new industries, cheap money, general prosperity, political advantages, and tends to bring about a rise in the value of securities and shares.

Planetary Values

Mars produces a feverish activity and much enterprise in the country, good trade and new flotations. But at the same time it incites to warlike feeling and intestine feuds and does not afford a very sound basis for operations. Its effect on the market depends on its aspects, and nature of the sign it occupies, but generally it induces to a brisk market, active buying, and a "bull" tendency. When falling in eclipse signs, i.e., with the Node, it induces a war, and thus creates an element of danger which is repeated on the markets by a fall in the value of stocks and shares.

Venus gives a peaceful condition of the country, quiet development of internal resources, plentitude of crops, and good security. Its effect on the markets is to produce a period of quiet inactivity, with few or no fluctuations.

Mercury brings a condition of nervous activity, much unrest, inconsequent talk, various rumours (according to its aspects) and a sense of instability. Quick buying and selling, scalping, and small but rapid fluctuations attend the influence of this volatile planet upon the markets.

A planet that is intrinsically evil in its effects, that is to say, one that depresses the market, may be rendered inoperative for the time being by good aspects from other planets, and also by the circumstance of it being in its own sign. But when badly aspected by any other planet, its effects will be detrimental to the financial interests of investors in such securities or shares as it may control.

We may now bring these general principles to the test by reference to published records, and for that purpose I have extracted my figures from the **Stock Exchange Intelligencer**, wherein they may be verified.

CHAPTER III.
EFFECTS OF TRANSITS.

It has been said that Saturn produces a depression in the value of securities controlled by the sign in which that planet is placed. Let us see if this be the fact or not. It is not necessary for the purpose of this enquiry to go further back than the half circuit of Saturn, which is about 15 years. If it produces marked effects in one half of the zodiacal circle it will do so in the other half. From like causes we argue like effects.

To go back then to the year 1898, when the planet Saturn was in the sign Sagittarius, against which we find the country of Spain indicated. The Government security on the open market is "Spanish 4% Sealed Bonds." Now, in April, 1898, Spain found herself suddenly plunged into a most unfortunate and, in fact, disastrous war with the United States of America. Writing of the malefic planets in Sagittarius in the pages of my journal, **Coming Events**, now unfortunately out of print, I specifically predicted this conflict between Spain and America. Its immediate effect on the markets was to cause a slump in "Spanish Fours." Before the war they were at 79, and after the war at 30—a fall of about 50 points per centum, which means a fortune to any who were able to utilise this foreknowledge. American Wheat went up with a bound, and continued to rise by daily and hourly leaps, from April 10th to May 3rd, when the "corner" so cleverly engineered by Jos. Leiter, Junr., collapsed owing to the appearance of the Spring crop rushed forward by Armour. When it is understood that 1d. per cental rise means £20 profit on a load of 4,800 Imperial Quarters, and that in this instance the price per cental rose 4s. 3d. per cental, from 7s. 6d. to 11s. 9d., it will be seen that the forecast of

Effects of Transits

INDICATIONS OF THE BURSTING

♉
♆
23

♌   Eclipse 28 ☽
♂ 23   ♒
☉ 28

♄ 23
♏

OF THE SOUTH SEA BUBBLE, 1720.

The Law of Values

this war was a thing of no small commercial value. A single load of wheat carried a profit of £1,020. At that time I wrote to Leiter and warned him of the futility of operating against celestial influences, and named May 3rd as the date at which the market would be against him if he continued to inflate prices. He dared it, and was caught in the trap he had set for others. The history of that sensational wheat deal would afford material for a drama. If thousands were ruined it was because they were ignorant of the Law of Values and were goaded on by their cupidity. To paraphrase an old saying: "Never speculate unless you know !"

We see, therefore, that Saturn gave Spain a serious time, which lasted until (in August) Senor Sagasta signed the Peace Treaty. The reconstruction of the National Debt, also predicted by me to the **Financial News**, took, place under the influence of the conjoined planets Uranus and Jupiter in Sagittarius in January following.

Saturn passed into the sign Capricornus in the year 1900, and this was accompanied by the great famine which threw the whole of the native industries into confusion, and resulted in the creation of a Mansion House Fund for the relief of the starving millions in India. The financial status of the country was not seriously affected, inasmuch as it was guaranteed by the British Government, but so far as the internal resources of the country were concerned, they were undoubtedly at the very lowest point. From Capricornus, the planet Saturn went into Aquarius, against which we find Russia indicated as being responsive to this sign. Saturn was in this sign in 1905, when the Russo-Japanese War broke out, in the course of which Russia lost its fleet and was forced to a treaty with its foes. Then followed the Insurrection and the terrible Red Sunday disaster, which had the ultimate effect of establishing the Duma or House of Public Representatives, the first indication of Reform in the annals of the Bureaucracy. The disgrace into which the Government had fallen by the overwhelming defeat at the hands of Japan gave the democratic element in Russia the opportunity for which it had long waited, to force important reforms, the chief being that of public representation.

Now when we turn to the financial effects of Saturn's

Effects of Transits

influence we find that between 1897, when the Government securities stood at their best, and 1906, when Saturn was affecting Russian affairs, there was a fall of from 30 to 60% in the value of securities. Thus in 1897 the 5% Loan stood at 154, in 1906 at 90 only. In 1896 the 4% Bonds stood at 105 and in 1906 at 71 only. In 1898 the 3% Bonds were at 96, and in 1907 at 61. In 1897 the 3½% Gold Loan stood at 103, and in 1906 it had fallen to 60. Thus on all sides and in all directions the influence of Saturn was marked by disaster, loss and depression.

From Aquarius Saturn passed into Pisces, against which we find Portugal. My readers must not think that it is put there to square with the facts. I did not myself make the discovery that Portugal responded to the sign Pisces, but I did in knowledge of that fact specifically predict the trouble that was to follow, and my predictions of revolution and violence were quoted by most of the leading newspapers, when the course of events gave them a curious value and interest.

In effect, Saturn in Pisces brought about the unrest in that country which culminated in the assassination of the King and the Crown Prince, which was immediately followed by a general revolution and the deposition and banishment of the young King.

In 1906 Portuguese Stock was at 72, and Saturn's influence in the sign Pisces was such as to bring it down to 58 in the year 1908. Writing in anticipation of the King's assassination, I was able to say, regarding the first week in February, that "the feature of the week will be the fall in Portuguese Stock." The tragic event took place on February 3rd. It is thus seen, not only that prediction is scientifically possible, but also that it may at times be made exceedingly profitable.

From Pisces Saturn went into the sign Aries, and the following years showed a succession of "lowest records" in the value of the prime security, Consols. Apropos of this the reader may note for himself the interview of **The Daily Mail** with the writer in the year 1898, when it was said that in the following year Consols would be "as much below par as they were then above it." In 1898 they stood at about 112, or 12 points above par. In 1890 they were at 88, or 12

The Law of Values

points below par. What I have myself succeeded in doing, others by the same method have done, and even more frequently, since they have in many instances nothing but money to think about.

The entry of Saturn into Taurus gave rise to the disturbances in Ireland over the Home Rule policy, considerable rioting, an almost unparalleled amount of crime, and a depreciation of land values. Persia meanwhile was in a state of insurrection, the Monarch being deposed and exiled. Its transit through Gemini will be reflected in America, Wales, and Egypt.

It is thus seen that there is a consistent record of misfortune and loss, traceable to the direct influence of Saturn in the different zones related to the several countries said to be ruled by them.

We may trace the same expansive effects due to the transits of Jupiter, and one example will serve for all others.

During the Russo-Japanese War referred to, Japanese Stock showed no such depression as that which affected Russian securities. In 1906, the 4½% Bonds were at 97, the highest point touched since the date of issue, and when Jupiter entered Libra in 1910 they rose to 102.

Similarly, the Mexican outbreak coincided with the transit of Uranus through the sign Capricorn in opposition to Neptune in Cancer; while the latter position fomented the democratic upheaval in China.

The countries governed by Gemini are Egypt, United States of America, and Wales, in all of which the depressing influence of Saturn will be felt in industrial and financial circles.

Meanwhile, the transits of Uranus and Jupiter through the sign Aquarius should be followed by financial reforms and development of trade in Russia and other parts ruled by that sign, leading to a general expansion of business, increased confidence, and a rise in the value of securities. It is to be observed, however, that this state of affairs is not likely to last, inasmuch as the planets Saturn and Uranus form their opposition in 1918-1919 from the signs Aquarius and Leo, while the eclipses begin to fall in these signs in

Effects of Transits

1915. Nevertheless the conjunction Uranus and Jupiter in the Spring of 1914 will have time to operate before these latter influences come into play, and hence 1914 should be a year of useful expansion and financial reform for Russia.

It has already been indicated that the position of the Node is of importance in tracing the occurrence of eclipses, and as these latter have an appreciable effect upon the fortunes of the various countries ruled by the signs in which they occur, I have thought it advisable to give the place of the Node for some years to come.

LONGITUDE OF NODE
JANUARY 1ST.

Year.	Ascen.	Node.	Descen.	Node.
1913	Aries	8	Libra	8
1914	Pisces	18	Virgo	18
1915	Aquarius	29	Leo	29
1916	Aquarius	10	Leo	10
1917	Capricorn	20	Cancer	20
1918	Capricorn	1	Cancer	1
1919	Sagittarius	12	Gemini	12
1920	Scorpio	22	Taurus	22

The approximate place of the Node for any month can be found by multiplying 1° 36' 40" by the number of months from January 1st, and subtracting the amount from the place shown in the above table. If a New Moon occurs within 18° 36' of the place of the Node, there will be an eclipse of the Sun. If a Full Moon occurs within 12° 24' of the Node, there will be an eclipse of the Moon, and the magnitude of the eclipse will be in inverse ratio to the distance. If within five degrees the eclipse will be total.

CHAPTER IV.
EFFECTS OF ASPECTS.

Except where the inherent natures of conjoined planets are mutually antagonistic, as Saturn and Mars, Neptune and Uranus, or Mars and Jupiter, we may consider the conjunction as being beneficial in its tendency.

Saturn and Uranus in conjunction produce wars and feuds, depress stocks and share values, and produce national calamities.

Saturn and Jupiter together bring about useful reforms, constitutional changes, and frequently produce the creation of funds.

Saturn and Mars bring wars, strife and upheavals, and always tend to depreciate securities.

Uranus and Jupiter bring about reforms and financial revisions, reconstruction of stocks and new share issues.

Uranus and Mars bring about insurrections and revolts, and disturb the existing order of things, thus depleting securities and deflating the markets.

Neptune and Jupiter produce unsound flotations, the creation of bogus funds, fraudulent schemes, and "rigging." Neptune in any configuration is to be mistrusted, as it tends to produce "wild-cat" schemes or downright frauds.

Mars and Jupiter bring about strong enthusiasms and demonstrations. So far as the markets are concerned, their influence is reflected in a strong "bull" tendency, highly speculative buying, and a run on stocks and shares governed by the sign they occupy.

Effects of Aspects

The opposition of the planets are uniformly evil in their effects upon securities, and a fall in the share values is always to be seen when the major planets oppose one another, as witness the recent oppositions of Uranus and Neptune in connection with the stocks and industrial shares of those countries under the influence of Cancer and Capricorn.

The quadratures are, of course, evil in their effects, as the trines and sextiles are good. But we lay chief stress upon the nature of the planet occupying a sign, for if Saturn be in a sign whatsoever, the securities related to that sign will not advance, even though Saturn may be well aspected. Taking, then, the simple natures of the planets in their action on the markets, it will be seen that:

Saturn produces depression.
Jupiter: Expansion.
Mars: Activity and enterprise, new developments and flotations.
Venus: Equable buying and selling.
Mercury: Nervousness or confidence, according to its aspect.

Eclipses, whether of the Sun or Moon in the several signs, have a detrimental effect on the value of securities governed by the sign in which the eclipsed luminary is posited. The positions of the eclipses can be traced by the longitude of the Node, for if the Moon's Node is in Aries, the eclipses will fall in Aries and Libra during that year, unless the Node is less than 12° 24' from either beginning or end of the sign. For an eclipse of the Moon cannot take place unless the Sun is within 12° 24' of the Node, while an eclipse of the Sun may occur when it is within 18° 36' of the Node. The recent eclipses in Taurus brought trouble upon Persia, Ireland, Italy and Morocco, and such interests as were financially represented on the markets suffered in consequence. The current eclipses falling in the signs Aries and Libra are calculated to bring trouble upon Japan, England, Peru, Argentina and Austria.

The motion of the Node is about 19° every year, and its motion is retrograde, that is, contrary to the order of the signs. Consequently the eclipses pass from Aries into Pisces, and

The Law of Values

DIAGRAM OF SIGNIFICATORS AT
OUTBREAK OF

♐
12° ♄ | ♅ 3°
staty. | staty.
Saturn | Uranus

♓   ♍

12° ♂ Mars

♊

THE HISPANO-AMERICAN WAR APRIL 6th, 1898.

Effects of Aspects

then to Aquarius, the limit of influence being 18 months in any sign. As eclipses have considerable effect upon the various territories denoted by the signs in which they fall, and consequently have a great deal of influence upon the price of stocks vested in those territories, I have endeavoured to make the location of them as simple and clear as possible.

CHAPTER V.
SENSITIVE POINTS.

There are two great circles called the meridian and horizon, which are related to the longitude and latitude of a place, and stand at right angles to one another. The meridian is that great circle which, when one is standing with his face to the South, where the Sun is about noon, passes immediately overhead from North to South cutting the horizon at right angles.

The horizon is that great circle which defines the limits of visibility.

The degree of the zodiac occupying the midheaven or meridian and that occupying the horizon, are sensitive points. It is found that the transits of the planets over these points are productive of very marked effects which influence the financial world to the greatest possible extent.

It is a matter of empiricism as to what degree holds the meridian, and consequently the horizon of various places. The following list may be taken as the result of experience.

	Midheaven	Ascend.
London...	♊ 9°	♍ 14°
St. Petersburg ...	♋ 9°	♎ 6°
Paris ...	♊ 11°	♍ 14°
Tokyo ...	♎ 29°	♑ 7°
Berlin ...	♊ 22°	♍ 24°
New York ...	♓ 24°	♋ 14°
Calcutta ...	♍ 7°	♐ 2°
Bombay ...	♌ 22°	♏ 20°
Sydney...	♏ 10°	♒ 16°
Rome ...	♊ 22°	♍ 23°

Sensitive Points

	Midheaven	Ascend.
Peking	♎ 6°	♐ 16°
Cape Town	♊ 27°	♍ 25°

It may be well to illustrate the working value of these observations, and I may take, therefore, one or two instances of the influence of transits of the major planets over these sensitive points of the zodiac.

In the year 1896 the malefic planets Uranus and Saturn were both in transit over the 20° of Scorpio, which is the ascendant of Bombay, and there began a most disastrous outbreak of Bubonic Plague in the Presidency which utterly demoralised trade in that important commercial centre, and caused the deaths of many thousands of victims. The year 1894 found Saturn in 29°♎, which is the midheaven degree of Tokyo, and the Chino-Japanese War was then in full play, Mars and Saturn forming an opposition in ♎/♈ 28°

The Boer War was begun on Oct. 11th, 1899, and on that date we find Neptune in ♊ 27°, which is the midheaven of Cape Town.

The Crimean War broke out on July 2nd, 1853, when Neptune was in 14° of Pisces, in exact opposition to the ascendant of the London horoscope. On January 25th, 1855, the Crimea scandal was ventilated in Parliament, and the Government was defeated. Saturn was then in ♊ 9°, the midheaven of London! The Transvaal War, of 1880, began on December 18th, when Uranus was stationary in exact conjunction with London's ascendant in ♍ 14°, and Mars in ♐ 9°, in direct opposition to the midheaven of London.

The Egyptian campaign and the fall of Khartoum, with the death of General Gordon, took place in 1884-5, when Saturn was in the midheaven of the horoscope of London, Saturn being in ♊ 9° in April, 1884. Gladstone's horoscope shows Saturn in opposition to the midheaven of the London horoscope, while the map for the execution of King Charles I, published by William Lilly, shows Saturn in ♊ 9°.

The reverses in Natal during the early stages of the Boer War, of 1899, were accompanied by the transit of Uranus over the opposition point to the midheaven of the London

The Law of Values

MALEFIC CONJUNCTION INDICATING

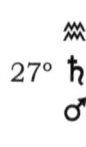

♒
27° ♄
♂

♉ —————————————|————————————— ♏

♌
THE RUSSO-JAPANESE WAR, 1905

Sensitive Points

horoscope, while at the same tune Saturn was in ♐ 27°, the opposition of the midheaven of Cape Town.

We cannot doubt, therefore, that Lilly was right in saying that the sign Virgo was the ascendant of the British Monarchy.

From this observation of William Lilly we see that a complete system of polarisations can be deduced, and the student of planetary influence will find that the great commercial centres of the world are influenced by the transit of major planets through the degrees occupying the midheaven and ascendant of the horoscopes, together with their oppositions, quadratures, trines and sextiles.

It should be observed, however, that the *stationary* positions of the major planets in these degrees are far more effective than mere transits, and great crises always attend the stay of a planet in a sensitive degree, *i.e.*, a degree occupying an angle of a horoscope.

CHAPTER VI.
HOW TO INVEST.

Taking it for granted that the reader has thoroughly tested the foregoing principles and has found them to be true in substance and fact, let us suppose that he has money to invest. His primary object will be to find a market in which he can buy at the lowest price with a fair degree of security, an adequate interest, and an opportunity of selling out at an advantage. It is in this latter operation that he may look for his greatest profits. First of all he should enquire whether the security is well founded, and readily dealt in on the open market. This information he can get from any broker or bank. To buy cheaply he must find a market which responds to the sign through which Saturn last made transit. Having taken up his stock, he will hold it until after Jupiter has made his transit through the same sign. He can then sell at the highest price that is likely to be touched during the space of 12 years.

Presuming that he holds some Peruvian Stock or Shares, it is obvious that he should clear these by selling them the moment Saturn enters Aries.

It is necessary that before buying stock, search should be made on the following points:

1. That no eclipses occur in the ruling sign of the stock during the period for which investment is proposed to be made.

2. That no transit of Saturn, Uranus or Neptune occurs in that sign during the period.

3. That Jupiter will pass through the sign during the period.

How to Invest

He will then buy and hold until after Jupiter has made his transit of the sign and sell at the best price obtainable in the open market. Thus, he buys after the transit of Saturn, and sells after the transit of Jupiter. He thus buys at the lowest and sells at the highest, taking his dividends in the meantime. So that whether a man is a buyer or seller of stock he has only to keep his eye upon the major planets and the eclipses and thus secure the best results. He must look to Saturn chiefly for depressions of the market and to Jupiter for inflation, but always considering the paramount effect of eclipses.

So far we have looked only on the problem from the point of view of the investor. The man who desires to speculate will have to abandon the sober rules of procedure given in these pages, and will have to avail himself either of his own intuitive acumen, or preferably of the specialised faculty of a financial agent. It is not proposed to disclose in this place the means whereby the daily fluctuations of the markets, whether in shares or produce, may be accurately foretold. These have reference to secondary causes and constitute the master-key to the Stock and Share market, which my correspondents make use of. I have contented myself in this place with the simple statement of certain primary laws, which, when properly understood, will instruct a man what to do and when to do it, so far as investment is concerned.

CHAPTER VII.
HOW TO AVERAGE.

When using the word average, we mean a point of value as nearly as possible between the highest and lowest prices of buying or selling. Thus, a man may buy £1,000 worth of Stock for £840, the price per £100 being thus £84. Should the Stock thereafter fall to £82 he may average by buying a further £1,000 of Stock at that price, and he thus reduces his buying price for the £2,000 worth of Stock to £83, and should it recover to £84 he can sell out at a profit, whereas otherwise he could not have sold for more than he gave.

Now this system of averaging can be usefully applied to the matter of investment in such manner as greatly to reduce the chances of a faulty investment. The process is to take the highest and lowest prices of a Stock or of Shares for each year during a period of seven or more years. These may be taken from the **Stock Exchange Intelligencer**, or any other authoritative record. The seven highest prices are then to be added together, as also the seven lowest prices. Each of these has then to be divided by the number of years to get the highest and lowest averages. The results are then added together and divided by two, which gives a true average, below which it is safe to buy under all normal conditions of the market. One or two examples will doubtless be of service :

Consolidated Annuities (Consols) 2½% Stock. Between 1895 and 1907 the highest was 114 in the year 1896, and the lowest was 80¾ in the year 1907. The average is thus for 12 years :

How to Average

INDICATIONS OF

```
                 ♓
            22° ♄
                ♂
    Ⅱ ─────────┼───────────── ♐
                │
                ♍
```

THE PORTUGUESE REVOLUTION.

The Law of Values

$$\begin{array}{rr} \text{Highest} \ldots & 114 \\ \text{Lowest} \ldots & 80\tfrac{3}{4} \\ \hline 2) & 194\tfrac{3}{4} \\ \hline \text{Average} \ldots & 97\tfrac{3}{8} \end{array}$$

This price would therefore be the true average value of Consols under normal conditions. The fact that it is not a safe investment at such a price is seen from the low record of 72¾ in the year 1912.

To correct for any given year we proceed as follows:

$$\begin{array}{rr} \text{Highest since 1907} & \\ \text{(June, 1908)} = & 88\tfrac{3}{8} \\ \text{Lowest since 1910} & \\ \text{(October, 1912)} = & 72\tfrac{3}{4} \\ \hline 2) & 161\tfrac{1}{8} \\ \hline \text{Average} & 80\tfrac{9}{16} \end{array}$$

In the abnormal conditions in which the British Government is working, it is safe to say that even this low average is not a safe buying point, and that recent eclipses in Aries and the transit of Saturn through that sign during 1908-10 have had, and will continue to have, a detrimental effect upon British securities. It will be observed that Saturn will be in transit over the midheaven of London in 1913, and in view of former experience of its dire influence, it is positively certain that British interests are to be jeopardised even more than they have been during the present regime.

Union Pacific Railroad Company.

$$\begin{array}{lr} \text{Highest 1895 to 1906,} & \\ \quad \text{inclusive (12 years)} & 203 \\ \text{Lowest do. do.} \ldots & 3\tfrac{1}{8} \\ \hline 2) & 206\tfrac{1}{8} \\ \hline \text{Average} & 103\tfrac{1}{16} \\ \text{Highest 1907-1910} \ldots \ldots & 225\tfrac{7}{8} \\ \text{Lowest } \text{''} \quad \text{''} \ldots \ldots & 107\tfrac{11}{16} \\ \hline 2) & 333\tfrac{9}{16} \\ \hline \text{Average} & 166\tfrac{3}{4} \end{array}$$

How to Average

Thus we have the following averages :

For 12 years 1895-1906 = $103_{1/16}$
For 4 years   1907-1910 = $166¾$
For 16 years 1895-1910 = 135

This is a fair average buying price in the present state of the market, which, however, is particularly nervous and "panicky." The forthcoming transit of Saturn through Ⅱ will disorganise American industries, and produce a heavy fall in the price of Stocks and Shares, so that investment is not to be recommended. The above examples will show, however, the process of finding investment buying and selling averages, under varying conditions, over a period of years.

Any assistance that may be required by readers, either concerning the interpretation of influence or the application of these principles to the exigencies of particular cases, can be had on application.

CHAPTER VIII.
CONSIDERATIONS.

Passing in review the various principles herein laid down for the guidance of investors, it should be first of all particularly noted that they apply exclusively to the problems of investment and not to the exigencies of successful speculation. The rules for this latter are as far sundered from the present method as horary astrology is from mundane, or chalk from cheese. It is confidently affirmed on the testimony of those who have followed the speculative method, that exact prediction of the in and out daily fluctuations of the markets can be as accurately foretold as the more extensive periodic depressions and elevations of values. All that I have sought to show in these pages is that a very definite effect upon the values of securities can be directly traced to the effect of planetary influence. I have also given some well-tried rules for the guidance of investors. It is possible to extend this instruction indefinitely, but if I have succeeded in placing the Law of Values on a sound cosmical basis, I have completed my task and there is nothing further to be said in the matter.

I look with considerable apprehension upon the trend of modern politics, and having in view the great cyclic law of periodicity, whereby the rise and fall of the great civilisations of the world have been hitherto determined, I am disposed to think that hereafter the greatness of our Empire can only be preserved by encouraging the closest possible relations with our various colonies, the extension of a preference system, and the most stringent methods of tariff reform. The signs of the times are dead against the ascendancy of insular British prestige, but as a mother lives again in her children or a tree in the fruit of its branches, so the

Considerations

INDICATIONS PREFIGURING THE MEXICAN OUTBREAK

♑
♅
22°
Uranus

♈

Mars ♂ 24°
☉ 22° ♎

♋ | Neptune
♆ 22°

AND
THE CHINESE REVOLUTION.

Law of Values

United Kingdom may continue. In this view I am sustained by the greatest of astrological Kabalists, Michael Nostradamus, who in his quatrains links the destinies of England with those of Spain, and although in his day no alliance had been made by England with the predominant power in Europe, yet it was by the alliance of the British Throne with Philip II of Spain, that England rose to a position of the first power in Europe, and although Nostradamus affirms that

> * Grand empire sera par l'Angleterre
> Le Pempotan plus de trois cents.

yet he sufficiently indicated that the period when

> " Her armies vast shall pass by land and sea,"

is limited to a period of something over 300 years, and that Spanish influence in Europe would proportionately decline.

Certain indications, too numerous and recondite to embody in an exposition of this sort, which have come to my notice, lead me to believe that the year 1913 is destined to bring about an international and political crisis in Europe, and it goes without saying that Great Britain, as a credit nation, cannot pass unhurt. My advice to investors is, therefore, to clear all Government securities and invest in Colonial Stocks, specially mentioning New Zealand and Canadian, and Mexican among the International securities. My reasons for this advice will, I think, sufficiently appear from a consideration of the principles expounded in this short treatise, and incidentally they will serve as a praxis from which the student of the Law of Values may know how to regulate his judgment.

As a consistent believer in the solidarity of the universe, in the fact of interplanetary action, and consequently in that of planetary influence in human life, I venture to believe that others, who view the facts displayed in these pages, will join with me in these beliefs, and I am convinced, from experience, that their adherence will not only be well-founded, but will, moreover, be a continual source of benefit to them. In such hope and belief I commend this treatise to their indulgent consideration.

---

* Great Empire to the English arms shall be
In fullest force three hundred years or more.

THE SILVER KEY

A GUIDE TO SPECULATORS

BY

SEPHARIAL

Author of
"The Manual of Astrology," **"Prognostic Astronomy**,"
"A Manual of Occultism," etc.

"The prince of English astrologers." - ***The Referee***
"The foremost living astrologer." - ***The Evening News***

"Who takes the tide takes all." - *Anon.*

"There is a tide in the affairs of men, which, taken at the flood, leads on to fortune." - *Shakespeare*

Publisher's Note

On times and calculations in this book.

On page 63 and elsewhere, you will find time given as 3.3, 4.6, 5.2, etc. I have seen this kind of time-keeping used in the UK. I believe these decimals represent tenths of an hour, e.g., 6 minutes, but have not gotten any of my UK friends to confirm. If true, then the figures above become 3:18, 4:36 and 5:12.

On page 78, using a noon ephemeris, Sepharial instructs how to calculate ascendants by adding TIME to SIDEREAL TIME. His results are correct, but his process is not clear. The correct procedure is to add LMT to Sidereal Time. Those who do not live in the vicinity of London should first reduce their clock time to LMT, before adding the Sidereal Time for the date in question. For those who live in other lands, there is a further small increment to be added (or subtracted) depending on how far east or west of Greenwich one may be. The exact instructions can be found in any good introduction to astrology, under the chapter entitled, "How to calculate a natal chart," or some such. A good computer program will of course produce accurate results with little effort.

As noted on pg. 76, 1 stone (st.) equals 14 lbs, or 6.35 kg.

David R. Roell

PREFACE TO SECOND EDITION

THE great demand which has been made for this work during recent months has suddenly exhausted the supply of what hitherto has been a somewhat obscure and neglected work. It has been found necessary to provide a further edition and the opportunity has been used to eliminate all matter which does not bear directly upon the main object of the work, while at the same time everything essential has been retained. The publication has led to many enquiries for a later and fuller expression of the principles contained in this work, but it has been found inconvenient and inadvisable to satisfy this demand except to a limited number of approved applicants under conditions which preclude resale or publication. I deem it right in this place to affirm that the "Silver Key" was not advanced as a "system," but was merely an attempt, along scientific lines, to answer the general question as to the possibilities of Astrology in connection with racing. Much research and observation has since been made and the highest possible consecutive series of winning results has been achieved. How far the subject has been carried only the favoured few are in a position to say. But as an introduction to the subject nothing better has ever been offered to the public than is to be found in these pages.

SEPHARIAL.

CONTENTS

INTRODUCTION	45
THE FUTURE METHOD	47
SCIENCE OF NUMBERS	51
SOME CONSIDERATIONS	55
NAMES AND NUMBERS	60
FINDING WINNERS	65
WINNING COLOURS	69
THE LUNAR KEY	75
HOW TO SET THE FIGURE	78
ELONGATION OF MOON	80
THE TEST	82
POLARITY	91
SELECTION	93
THE ASPECTS	94
FAVOURITES	97
GRAVITY AND EVOLUTION	98
A CALCULATOR	100
SOMETHING TO COME	103
A WARNING	105
ON SPECULATION	107
CONCLUSION	111
TABLES OF SIDEREAL TIMES	112
TABLES OF ASCENDANTS	115

INTRODUCTION

IN the following pages I have endeavoured to set forthwith as much particularity as the case demands, several systems that have been advanced with a view to solving the problem of successful speculation. In the first instance, I have propounded a general question as to the possibility of "figuring" successfully on future events, and have added a note of warning to those who are young in experience, and ignorant of professional methods and decoys.

In regard to the application of numbers and colours to turf problems, I need only say here that there is more in them than may at first be recognised, and as they have a bearing upon the general scheme of this book, I have introduced them without the guarantee of personal experience or recommendation. The reader may vex himself with them or not as he pleases.

The main purpose of this book is to demonstrate, beyond all doubt or cavil, that the Moon, which plays such an important part in natural phenomena, and which, on that account, is rightly accorded a premier position in all astrological considerations, is the *Silver Key* to successful speculation. If we stood in need of an à *priori* reason for considering the lunar orb as having a controlling influence in what we rightly call "sub-lunary" affairs, we find it in that heaping-up of the ocean waters which we know as high tide.

The credit of having first defined the cause of the tides rests with Kepler, who propounded an entirely new system of astronomy which bears his name. To him also stands the credit of a frank avowal of his belief in planetary influence in human life, a belief that was grounded in experience, for he says, "An unfailing experience of the course of mundane events *in harmony with the changes occurring in the heavens* has instructed and compelled my unwilling belief."

Kepler affirmed that the tides were due to the combined action of the Sun and Moon upon the Earth's waters, the attraction of the Moon being considerably greater than that of the Sun. Air being lighter than water, and its surface being much nearer to the Moon than of the ocean, there can be no doubt that the lunar orb exercises a very great influence upon it, and causes much higher tides in the air than in the sea. Recent scientific observations have shown that there is also an earth-tide due to the action of the luminaries.

It is along these lines that my researches have been directed, and, in effect, I am able to demonstrate that the Moon's influence extends to matters of a nature quite removed in the ordinary mind from considerations of gravity in every sense of the word, and which, in fact, are usually regarded as purely speculative, and attributable to quite other causes than those suggested in this place. In a word, I have succeeded in finding a key to the vexed problem of speculative finance; and its application to turf results is resorted to in this instance merely because of the facility of illustration afforded by the published records. The argument and proof might as readily have been drawn from the rise and fall of share values on the Stock Exchange, or the price of articles in the produce markets, such as tea, coffee, sugar, wheat, etc., but the illustration would not have been so popular nor the proofs so easily examined.

If I carry my principal point, that of planetary influence in mundane affairs, I shall quite cheerfully risk the possible accusation of trafficking in things which are *infra dignitate*, as perhaps are most things that are under the Sun.

SEPHARIAL.

THE SILVER KEY

THE FUTURE METHOD

I WONDER how many of my readers really believe in luck, or could define exactly what they mean by that term, as applied to games and sports of a speculative character where the forecasting of events is a matter of importance ?

The man who follows racing, at all events, seems to take luck as a sort of third term in a doubtful equation somewhat as follows:—

> AS FORM *IS TO* FANCY
> *SO IS* LUCK *TO THE RESULT.*

Nobody seems seriously to have considered that there may be a definite law at work in these things, inconsiderable as they are in relation to the destiny of humanity as a whole.

But Nature does not suffer from neglect. She is well able to take care of herself and to mother the rest of us into the bargain. The fact that men ignore her teachings does not one whit affect the net result of her operations. It is we alone who suffer. Her first lesson in the power of numbers and ratios was given in the foundations of the solar system, it was continued in the production of the first snowflake, in the crystallisation of the minerals, and in numerous other ways. The fault is ours, and ours the penalty, if these teachings have been disregarded.

The reckless sportsman backs his "fancy" against the field. Others, more amenable to reason, follow "form," and resort to cover where danger is shown. Both go down sooner or later. And why ?

The Silver Key

In the first place the man who backs his fancy without anything else to show for it is like one who embarks without rudder or compass. He is bound to find the rocks ! On the other hand the man who follows form ignores the fact that it is a variable quantity. A horse has as much right to feel "not quite so fit to-day" as has the trainer, the jockey or the common stable boy. If horses could speak they would give us some good reasons, no doubt, for each and all of their failures. Besides, is it not a fact that favourites and winning jockeys of one season are often negligible quantities in the next, while always there are new surprises cropping up to illustrate the paradox that in every race there is always one that is better than the best ?

Now I am not a Daniel come to judgment, and what I have to say, although entirely new to the bulk of the racing world, I have consistently maintained and advocated for the past twenty-five years. In a word, I regard "Chance" and "Luck" as terms used to cloak our ignorance of natural laws and affirm that planetary influence is at the root of every mundane event. Geometry and the science of numbers will compass every turf result and every market movement. In proportion as we increase our knowledge of these factors we eliminate the element denominated chance.

Before presuming to approach the public with a statement of planetary influence as applied to common events of the day, such as turf results, market movements, etc., I submitted my claim to a succession of very severe tests with men of high standing in the racing and commercial worlds. In the matter of racing I succeeded in establishing a record in the art of finding winners.

In 1907 I walked in on the Editor of **Sporting Sketches** and submitted to a test on the instant, finding five winners and a walk-over out of six events that day. On a consecutive test extending over six weeks from May 5th to June 15th inclusive, submitted to some of the staff of **The Racing World**, the results were 98 wins and 60 losses out of 158 events or about 62 per cent. results. On a flat stake of £1 the credit weekly balance varied from £21 to £50.

But what of those 60 losers ? More than forty were

The Future Method

accounted for as soon as the actual runners were known, for I was not working on the tape or on the course, but with the ordinary and imperfect information contained in the morning papers. The rest, amounting to upwards of a score of losers, I put down to my ignorance.

Yet for a long run 62 per cent. of wins is a record which no newspaper tipster has come near at any time. From March 18th to May 18th, 1907, "The Scout" of the **Daily Express** scored 63 points, while in the same period every other newspaper *lost* from 15 to 63 points on a flat stake. Compared with these results Astrology makes an easy first in the field. The results of a flat stake of £1 during the weeks under test were as follows :—

Week ending	Races.	Won.	£	s.	d.	
May 11, 1907	24	14	45	17	2	gained
„ 18, 1907	20	12	38	18	0	„
„ 25, 1907	31	22	49	14	6	„
June 1, 1907	37	25	44	4	0	„
„ 8, 1907	19	10	21	0	0	„
„ 15, 1907	27	15	39	0	0	„
	158	98	238	13	8	

Is there any other method in existence which can show over 50 per cent. winners for a consecutive month ? All sorts of schemes are before the public for making turf transactions a profitable form of investment, but they presume that the man who uses a numerical progression, or any other approved method, has the ability for finding winners. In point of fact, these so-called systems are based on selections from "form" and on a flat stake they are bound to spell loss. I ignore form and have no sort of fancy. I am guided entirely by weights and do not require to know what horse may carry the weight I want. Hence, in the course of the 1907 season there were some nice long-priced winners to my credit, as Ob, 28/1 (S.P. 25/1) ; Father Blind, 20/1; Dark Ronald, 33/1 ; Lally, 100/8 ; Maya, Auber and many others, 100/8, etc. To the general question : Can astrology find winners ? I answer, most emphatically, Yes. Except in the interests of astrology I am not desirous of blowing my trumpet, but I think—nay, I know—that there is no newspaper prophet who can attempt anything of a like nature with a shadow of a chance of beating astrology out of doors. It is well to remember in this connection that "form," the sheet-anchor of the professional tipster and the mainstay of the book-maker, does not enter into the equation. Did it do so, we should not have had the gratification of seeing Father Blind win the Great Metropolitan Stakes. Indeed, what is known as form is a variable quantity, and, alas, for the prophets and their followers, too often a minus one. Luck, in the purely fortuitous sense, we do not believe in. But when we affirm, as constantly we do in the statement of astrological principles, that the world is governed by numbers, we are making no sort of claim on people's credulity. For, although they may not follow us into the ramifications of astrology, they are at all times well able to see for themselves that everything in Nature bears us out. When the great Greek philosopher said; "God geometrises," he was stating a self-evident truth, a truth that is evident at all events to those who have studied the traceries in the great book of life. See what a great variety of beautiful forms the snowflakes take. They are nevertheless all formed by angles of sixty degrees—the sextile aspect in astrology, the angle at which water always crystallises. All the superior metals crystallise at the angle or complemental angle of any regular polygon that may be inscribed in a circle. From the snowflake to the stellar universe the step is not a hand's breadth. The manual of the Great Architect covers all. "As above, so below," and everywhere law, order, symmetry and number. To the extent that we are able to understand and apply the laws of the universe to the incidents of life, we obliterate chance and reduce speculation.

THE SCIENCE OF NUMBERS

From time immemorial the virtue and power of Numbers has been the theme of every philosopher to whom the world has paid honours. Beginning in the Far East under the benign sovereignty of the Yellow Emperor some thousands of years before the present era, and continuing through the Creton philosopher, Pythagoras, and that famous Arabian astronomer, Albumazer, to times which are comparatively modern, we find the Kabalists from Hiram Abif to Rosenrath, the Rosicrucians and the Hermetist of the Dark Ages, down to the days of Paracelsus and the modern Cagliostro, extolling the science of numbers. Even the great scientist Mendelieff recognised the saying of Pythagoras, that "God geometrises," to be a true one, and in his famous table of the numerical ratios of the elements he observes a species of Kabalism which cannot be otherwise described than as a supreme piece of intelligent anticipation.

But by the science of numbers one does not infer merely the use of arithmetical processes as in addition, subtraction and proportion, but also and more particularly the relationship of quantities and values to the active principles in nature which they are held to represent, and of which figures are but the symbols.

The active principles in persons and things are those which are implanted by nature through the instrumentality of planetary influence. This appears to be recognised by John Haydon in "The Holy Guide," where he ascribes certain numbers, representing as many principles, to the various planets thus:—

The Number of Saturn is 8.
        Do.   Jupiter is 3.
        Do.   Mars is 9.
        Do.   Sun is 1, and also 4.
        Do.   Venus is 6.
        Do.   Mercury is 5.
        Do.   Moon is 2, and also 7.

Taking the numbers in their order, 1 represents Origin; 2, Reflection; 3, Creation; 4, Formation; 5, Germination; 6, Production; 7, Satisfaction; 8, Destruction ; 9, Distribution.

Each planet is said to rule a day of the week, to which it gives its name, and there is perhaps no more wonderful fact in the whole range of human polity than that every nation of whatever age or country has agreed to this tradition, plotting out the week into seven periods of equal length, and ascribing them to the same planetary names in the same succession.

The reason of this arbitrary distribution of the members of the solar system through the days of the week was not at once apparent to antiquarians, who found in it no correspondence with the natural order of things. But when, on reference to the old astrological authors, it was found that there was a further distribution of the same planets through the twenty-four hours of the day, the reason for the names and succession of the days of the week was at once apparent.

Beginning with Sunday as the first day of the week, the Sun ruled the first hour after sunrise. Venus the next, then Mercury, the Moon, Saturn, Jupiter and Mars in succession; the same order being repeated from the 8th to the 14th hour, and so on throughout the day. And as there are twenty-four hours in the day and seven planets in the system, it follows that the succession will be repeated three times, leaving three hours to continue in the fourth series. Thus on Sunday, the Sun rules the first hour after sunrise, and is repeated in the 8th hour and the 15th, and the day is then completed in the following order:—

The Science of Numbers

Sunday—15th hour ruled by Sun			
	16th „	„	Venus.
	17th „	„	Mercury,
	18th „	„	Moon.
	19th „	„	Saturn.
	20th „	„	Jupiter.
	21st „	„	Mars.
	22nd „	„	Sun.
	23rd „	„	Venus.
	24th „	„	Mercury.

Monday, 1st hour, ruled by Moon.

Thus the Moon, which gives its name to Monday, succeeds in natural order to the rulership of the first hour after sunrise on the second day of the week. Thus it is to astrology we must turn for an explanation of the commonest fact in the world's history, the naming of the days of the week. The Chaldeans, apparently, were responsible for this planetary distribution, and in illustration of these preliminary comments, I shall show experimentally that purely astrological considerations influenced them in these ascriptions. Perhaps the fact that these astrological divisions of time are to-day extensively used for the purpose of bringing the "laws of chance" under control, and proving that sound and number, following planetary influence, play an important and perhaps a paramount part in racing results will suffice to command the attentive interest of my readers.

Having shown how the week and the day are divided into planetary periods of days and hours, it remains to be shown how in similar manner the hour is so divided. Each hour of 60 minutes is divided into 15 parts of 4 minutes each. The Chinese call these periods *siaou-ki*, and the Hindoos know them as *trims' āmshas*, *i.e.*, one-thirtieth part of an *āmshas* or sign of the zodiac, since one degree or thirtieth part of a sign passes over the meridian in 4 minutes of time.

Thus on Saturday the first hour is ruled by Saturn. This hour of Saturn is then divided into 15 parts of 4 minutes each, the first part or period being ruled by Saturn, the next by Jupiter, followed by Mars, the Sun, Venus, Mercury and the Moon. Saturn again succeeds and rules the eighth hour,

Jupiter the ninth, and so on. The fifteenth period is again ruled by Saturn (on a Saturday), and the next planet Jupiter thus succeeds to the first period in the next hour which is ruled by Jupiter.

We see, then, that the planet which gives its name to the day rules the first hour of that day, and that the planet which gives its name to the hour rules the first period of that hour. The application of these divisions of time to the business in hand—that of finding winners—has been partially explained by S. H. Ahmad in **"The Mysteries of Sound and Number**,*"* to which the reader is referred, but it is safe to say in regard to that preliminary statement of the law, that it has since been improved out of existence by further study on the part of its exponent and of other students.

SOME CONSIDERATIONS

In continuation of what has been said about the Alphabetical System of evaluation in relation to turf results, I may now offer some explanations and suggestions, which, if they do not materially assist the reader, will at all events serve to show where pitfalls are likely to be encountered.

In the first place it should be known that the method of ascribing certain values to the planets is of occidental origin, being in fact indigenous to the Kabalism of the Rosicrucians and Hermetists. On the other hand the system of dividing time by periods of four minutes is Oriental. This period represents the thirtieth part of a sign of the zodiac which passes over the meridian in four minutes of time. They do not refer to the horizontal rising of the signs at all, and therefore cannot be legitimately referred to local sunrise.

Admitted that every sound has a numerical value, and the Kabalists have always affirmed this as a fact, it will be seen that every name must therefore be a composite of sound-values, and these values when added together will give a sum which, being reduced to its lowest or unit value, must coincide with the value of a planet, which is always expressed in units.

According to the rules, certain letters syncopate and others are doubled, while some consonants have a single or a double value. My own view will be found in a subsequent chapter. In effect, however, we find that by whatever system of evaluation we employ, every name comes to have a certain value, and consequently the unit values of all names of competitors will range from 1 to 9. The difficulty of applying this fact to the problem in hand is one that has been freely expressed and appears to arise from the variations of pronunciation prevailing in different parts of the country.

The Silver Key

In regard to foreign names, it is essential that the correct pronunciation should be obtained from one who knows the language to which it belongs. Take, for instance, such names as Dieudonné, sire of Adeodatus; Aboyeur, Arcis sur Aube, Atteloigna, Voyageuse, Ben Chouzié, Fléche, Ceiriog, Feu de Joie, Gentile, Cheveux, Kosciusko, L'Enseigne, Louvois, Loup Chien, etc., to give only a few examples. One has only to hear these names sounded variously by men in the street to be assured that the matter of coding names is no small business to those who have no knowledge of foreign languages.

Granted that one may obtain the true values of names, and a necessary correspondence of unit values with planetary values, there remains the difficulty of guessing the off time. In big events, where the competitors are numerous, the difficulty of fair starting is so great that there is often a difference of over twenty minutes between the set time and the off time of a race. The majority of events can, however, be fairly well accommodated to the system on the course. Off the course, it only adds one more to the many doubtful factors upon which to speculate.

Another difficulty that the student of the Alphabetical System will encounter is that, by the system of planetary periods there is a repetition of influence every sixteen minutes, or rather there is a succession of three periods of four minutes each followed by one that is neutral, and then these are repeated throughout the day. Thus, beginning with Saturn and its alternate Sun, we follow with the planet Jupiter and its alternate Venus, then by Mars and its alternate Mercury, and then by the Moon alone. After this period the same sequence recurs continually. Then, since all the numbers 8, 4/1, 3, 6, 9, 5, 7/2, are contained in sixteen minutes, and all the horses must code to one of these nine units, a large race presents the large majority of the competitors included in one of the first three periods or an interval of twelve minutes. Consequently, if you are wholly ignorant of the form of the competitors and have no "tips" by which to guide your judgment, the chances of finding a winner are exceedingly remote.

A further difficulty arises from the fact that any planet can win under its own number, or that of its alternate planet,

Some Considerations

or again under the number answering to the ruler of the sign in which it is found at the time. Thus to take an example : April 16th, 1908, planets situated as follows:—

> Saturn in Aries ruled by Mars 9. Own number 8. Alternate 4/1.
> Jupiter in Leo ruled by Sun 1. Own number 3. Alternate 6.
> Mars in Gemini ruled by Mercury 5. Own number 9. Alternate 5.
> Venus in Gemini ruled by Mercury 5. Own number 6. Alternate 3.
> Mercury in Aries ruled by Mars 9. Own number 5. Alternate 9.
> Sun in Aries ruled by Mars 9. Own numbers 4/1. Alternate 8.
> Moon in Libra ruled by Venus 6. Own numbers 7/2.

It is obvious, therefore, that the Alphabetical System presents many difficulties and as a system of selection could hardly be relied upon, although as illustrating the existence of a law of Correspondence between sound-values, numbers and planets, it will be found to be largely supported by results.

Here it is necessary to point the fact that this will be found most uniformly the case in all events which take place about the latitude of Greenwich, whether in East or West longitude. In other latitudes it cannot be the case if the basis of the calculation is the time of sunrise. It would be quite correct if the time were taken from the Sun's meridian passage. But owing to the obliquity of the zodiac in reference to the horizon of various localities, it will be found that at midsummer the Sun rises at York, which is 4m. 19s. West, sooner than it does on Greenwich by nearly 10 minutes, and that Liverpool, which is 11m. 58s. West, sees the Sun only two minutes later than Greenwich at the same season. At another time of the year the Sun rises on Liverpool 22 minutes after it rises on Greenwich. These facts clearly show that if calculation is to be made from sunrise, then the latitude of the place has to be taken into account when equating local time to Greenwich time for the purpose of this calculation. It is only twice a year, namely, at the equinoxes, that we can truly say the Sun rises on York 4m. 19s. later than Greenwich, and on Liverpool 11m. 58s. later.

These considerations have led me to invent and formulate a method that is correctly astronomical, which employs the actual positions of the chief cosmic factors, and which is a true system of selection, and not merely one of elimination.

This system may be called the Gravity System, inasmuch as it employs the same factors and follows the same principle as is expressed in the law governing the tides. In being critical in regard to other methods than my own, I do not wish to be destructive of anything that is based upon true principles. My aim is rather to be constructive, both as regards the detached materials of systems that are faulty, and as regards anything else, that may be considered preferable.

It appears to me that a true system should point you to one, or at most, two horses which can be safely invested upon in a majority of instances taken consecutively. When we have exhausted the significance of names and numbers there still remains weight. This factor I have succeeded in employing in a manner not hitherto expressed, and it is satisfactory to know that it is in agreement with a clearly understood and well-defined law, which anybody can observe in operation day after day.

In this system we get rid of several ambiguous factors, such as the coding of names, the alteration of planetary opposites, the off time of a race, considerations of form, distance, ground condition, jockeyship, etc., and rely entirely on the indication from weight, and the set time of the race; and these factors are taken in regard to the relative positions of the Sun and Moon, as regards the place for which calculation is made.

In regard to the system expounded in "The Mysteries of Sound and Number," it is to be observed that the planetary numbers were given out by Godfridus and Haydon together with those of the signs, which enter into another system of similar nature published by Mr. Erskine in "Law *versus* Chance." These values are traditional with the Kabalists. The system of time division into four minute periods is of Oriental origin. The credit of having combined the two and

Some Considerations

of employing them in the demonstration of the relations of sound and number is due to Mr. S. H. Ahmad. It is obvious, however, that "The Mysteries" contains only a preliminary statement of the law. The book was evidently written in the belief that planetary influence and the power of numbers lay at the root of apparently chance happenings, and this is undoubtedly the fact.

Before entering upon an exposition of the gravity system, it will probably be of interest to examine one or two other methods which have been advanced, as showing the relations of number and colour to the problems of speculation.

NAMES AND NUMBERS

I have now reached a point in my discussion of this question of finding winners when something of a more constructive nature may be attempted. There are before the world at the present time a number of systems, many of which are purely mathematical, some astronomical, and others kabalistic.

It would not be either possible or politic to discuss the relative merits of these various systems, but some hints may be given regarding the kabalistic sound and number systems which appear to have a basis in truth.

My readers will remember what has been said about the impossibility of using any system of sound-values which is so problematical as that which I have just dismissed, owing to the fact that no two students will agree as to computation of such values. To take only one concrete instance of this, I may say that I was in the company of two students of this method only the other day, and I was informed that a certain horse had formerly won as a 7, also as an 8 and a 3, while two of those present agreed that the horse's name was of the value of 5, and that it had won under that number.

My own view of the matter is that every letter which contributes to the sound-value of a name should be taken into account at its true value, for although certain letters are not sounded and therefore are omitted from the sound-value by some exponents, they should nevertheless be included, inasmuch as they modify the sound of other letters in the name, and, therefore, contribute to the general result. Thus, in the name of Pillo, the double L should be repeated, as Pilo is not the same thing, and the LL double letter modifies the value of the stressed vowel, and has there-

Names and Numbers

fore a value of 6 instead of 3.

The method which I now propose to introduce as a good specimen of the kabalistic systems that are rife observes this rule, and also has a constant value for each letter, the Hebraic values being followed.

The Alphabet is thus disposed
1—stands for A, Y, I, Q, J.
2— " B, K, R, C.
3— " G, L, S, or Sh.
4— " D, M, T.
5— " E, N, H (not aspirate).
6— " W, V, U.
7— " Z, 0, X (initial)
8— " H (aspirate), X (other than initial), and F.

The factors employed are:—
1.—The name of the place where racing occurs.
2.—The day planet.
3.—The hour planet.
4.—The names of the horses contesting an event.

The day and hour values are reduced to a single table, as follows:—

	Sun.	Mon.	Tue.	Wed.	Thu.	Fri.	Sat.
Saturn	4	0	3	0	9	9	0
Jupiter	5	1	4	1	1	1	1
Mars	4	0	3	0	9	9	0
Sun	4	9	3	9	9	9	9
Venus	8	4	7	4	4	4	4
Mercury	7	3	6	3	3	3	3
Moon	2	7	1	7	7	7	7

The method of procedure is thus:—

Lincoln, 18th March, 1907, Monday.

1.—Take the value of the place of meeting.

Example. — Lincoln = 3152735 = 26 = 8. The values of all the principal places can be computed and arranged in order for reference on occasion.

The Silver Key

2.—The day is Monday, and the planetary hour is also that of the Moon at 1:45 p.m., which was the time of the first race. This according to the above table gives the value of 7.

3.—The winner of the race was Java, value 1161 = 9.

Collecting the three values, we have

Lincoln	=	8
Monday Moon	=	7
Java	=	9
Sum	..	24

Rejecting the nines, i.e., dividing by 9, we have the unit value of 6.

It is now necessary to state that the winning numbers are 1, 3, 6, 7, and 9. The number 5 can also win when it is the sum of all the factors, or when it is the result of 14, but not when reduced from 23.

The losing numbers are 2, 4, and 8.

The relative value of the winning number is not constant, but there is a rule which tells us when 1 is to be preferred to a 3 or a 7 in the same race, and so of other numbers.

For the purpose of illustration, the planetary hours of the 18th of March, 1907, London, are set out in order so far as they cover the times of the races on that date.

PLANETARY HOURS.

1.1 to 2.1 ruled by	Moon	—7
2.1 to 3.2 " "	Saturn	—0
3.2 to 4.2 " "	Jupiter	—1
4.2 to 5.3 " "	Mars	—0

A planetary table should be prepared as a preliminary to the calculation of an event.

Against the successive hours are set the planetary values for those hours on Monday from the table of day and hour values given in the above table. We have also the constant value of Lincoln=8.

All that is now necessary to complete the calculations for successive events is to find the name-values of the horses,

Names and Numbers

conveniently noting first of all such as stand foremost on form or current racing intelligence.

The off-time of the race is the time for which the calculation is made, and only on rare occasions is it the occasion of doubt, as when the set time is close to the end of a planetary hour.

The remaining events for the 18th March, 1907 were as follows:—

    2:20 Hour of Saturn   —0
    (Off 2:24)   Lincoln   —8
    Won by The Kicker   —
    485 212252=31   = 4
                                       12 = 3

    2:55 (3.3), Hour of Jupiter   —1
                         Lincoln   —8
    Won by Early Bird   —
    51231 2124=21   = 3
                                       12 = 3

    3:30 (3:37), Hour of Jupiter   —1
                          Lincoln   —8
    Won by Honest Bill   —
    755342133=33   = 6
                                   15 = 6

    4.0 (4.6), Hour of Mars   —0
                       Lincoln   —8
    Won by Claudian   —
    23164115=23   = 5
                                13 = 4

    4:30 (4:31), Hour of Mars   —0
                          Lincoln   —8
    Won by Zinc   —
    7152=15   = 6
                       14 = 5

    5.0 (5.2), Hour of Mars   —0
                     Lincoln   —8
    Won by Molly Shiels   —
    47331 31533=33   = 6
                                 14 = 5

With the exception of the 4.0 race, it will be seen that all the results fall into line with the requirements of the method, and incidentally the last two races are illustrations of 5 being a winning number when derived from 14.

Now let us take the Lincolnshire Handicap for 1906, 1907, and 1908, in terms of these rules. The race in each year was at 3.20 p.m., on a Tuesday, but the "off" times were different. There was also a slight variation in the planetary hours due to difference of dates, but in each case it was the hour of Venus. Lincoln we know equals 8. The hour of Venus on Tuesday =7.

1906-3:20 (3:51), 27th March.
Hour of Venus —7
Lincoln —8
Ob=72 = 9
24 = 6

1907-3:20 (3:47), 19th March.
Hour of Venus —7
Lincoln —8
Ob=72 = 9
24 = 6

1908-3:20 (3:30), 24th March.
Hour of Venus —7
Lincoln —8
Kaffir Chief —
218812 28158=46 = 1
16 = 7

These results are uniform and satisfactory. The system, however, has one apparent drawback, one that was lodged in a certain connection against the alphabetical method, namely, that all the horses' names must code to a value of from 1 to 9, and the results must come out as winning under 1, 3 (5), 6, 7, or 9; or losing under 2, 4 (5), and 8 ; and of those which come out under the winning numbers several may be alike in value, so that some law of precedence must avail to determine which of them is to be preferred. Those who, being versed in kabalism, are also capable of appreciating astronomical factors, will not hesitate, but will know how to choose between them.

FINDING WINNERS

In illustration of one or two points raised in the consideration of the Kabalistic system of enumeration set out in our last chapter, it is of first importance that the true time of sunrise at the locality of racing should be known, as this is the basis of the planetary hour. The time from sunrise to sunset being divided by 12 gives the planetary hours for the day, while the period from sunset to sunrise similarly divided gives the hours for the night. But owing to difference of longitude and latitude between various places, the duration of the day will vary according to the season of the year.

During the summer the Sun rises earlier and sets later than the almanack time to places that are north of Greenwich, and in winter the reverse. Thus Lincoln, which is practically on the Greenwich meridian, will see the Sun rising earlier and also setting later than Greenwich during the season between March 21st and September 22nd, because it is more northerly. In the winter, between September 22nd and March 21st, it is the reverse of this.

The following easy equation of the time of sunrise may be useful:

I. Find the ascensional difference of the Sun under the latitude of Greenwich and that of the locality in question.

RULE.—Tangent of latitude of place multiplied by the tangent of the Sun's declination equals the sine of the ascensional difference.

Example.—Find the difference of sunrise at Lincoln on Midsummer day (June 21st), the Sun's declination on that day being 23° 27' N.

Lincoln is	53° 14' N.,	Log. tang.	10.12657
Sun's declin.	23.27 N.,	" "	9.63726
Ascen. Diff.	35° 29'	Log. sine	9.76383
London is	51° 32' N.,	Log. tang.	10.09991
Sun's declin.	23.27' N.,	" "	9.63726
Ascen. Diff.	33° 6'	Log. sine	9.73717

The difference between 35° 29' due to Lincoln, and 33° 6' due to London, is 2° 23' which, multiplied by 4, gives 9 mins. 32 secs., by which the Sun rises upon Lincoln earlier, and sets upon Lincoln later, than it does on London at this date, practically ten minutes.

Time of Sunrise at Greenwich   3:44 a.m.
                                      less 10
Time of Sunrise at Lincoln   3:34 a.m.

Thus it is seen how the day is a little longer than 19 minutes on June 21st, and the same amount shorter on December 21st at Lincoln than at Greenwich.

My friends "way up North" need not unduly rejoice in the fact that their summer days are longer for it is counteracted by the fact that the Sun's altitude is so much less and its power thereby so much the weaker than here.

The law of compensation is always at work; a fact which Emerson was fond of driving home to all who were unduly elated or cast down.

But to return to our names and numbers. A useful illustration of the value of this kabalism was shown on one occasion when the indicated horses were College and Verdy, the weights being indistinguishable. The computation was as follows:—

It was at Newmarket, on Thursday, 23rd April, in the Column Product Stakes' race of one mile. The choice lay between Verdy and College, and although the latter was not tipped or fancied for the event it had a chance on the weights. The computation was as follows:

Finding Winners

```
Newmarket — 556412254 = 34      =7
Thursday in the hour of Mars    =9
Verdy =65241= 18                =9
                                ──
                                25 = 7

Newmarket — 556412254 = 34      =7
Thursday in the hour of Mars    =9
College =2733535 =28            =1
                                ──
                                17 = 8
```

Here the indication by named values favoured Verdy, but denied success to College, who came in third to Verdy and Mariotto.

But it is for this very reason of 17=8 being a losing number according to the Kabala, that one would have rejected Dean Swift in the City and Suburban. Thus:—

```
Epsom .. = 58374=27             =9
Wednesday in hour of Moon       =7
Dean Swift=451536184            =1
                                ──
                                17 = 8
```

And from this it appears that the mystic Kabala is not consistent. But it is yet a curious fact that the same number won the previous race in the same planetary hour, viz:—

```
Epsom .. = 58374=27             =9
Wednesday in hour of Moon       =7
Perdiccas =825412213            =1
                                ──
                                17 = 8
```

This seems to point to the probability that certain numbers are related to certain hours, and under particular conditions, relative to the positions of the planets at those hours, such numbers may win. It is nevertheless a fact that all the other results of this day's racing are in accord with the postulate that certain numbers are winning numbers.

The results are as follows :—

1:30—	won under	6—correct
2.5 —	”	”	1— ”
2:40—	”	”	8—wrong
3:15—	”	”	8— ”
3:50—	”	”	3—correct
4:25—	”	”	6— ”

I have now said enough about this method to give such of my readers as are interested in these curious studies an opportunity of testing it for themselves, and I think I am safe in saying they will find in it a pleasant pastime and not nearly so difficult a task as finding the winner. Like most numerical systems it does not materially aid in that direction, but if it is instrumental in keeping one off losers, that is perhaps as much as can be said for it in its present stage of development.

WINNING COLOURS

How many people are there, I wonder, who are altogether blameless of superstitious reverence for colours, or who can claim immunity from the seductive influence of a good thing in silks ? When this means the right man up—a good jockey in the sporting colours of a good owner—it is well-nigh irresistible. **The Daily Express** informs us that lucky colours are all the fashion, and it would appear that a certain fashionable dressmaker and milliner has reduced the thing to a science.

Nowadays your wife's dress must be not only of the correct cut and material, but also of the correct colour, which, in a word, is the dominant planetary colour of the month in which she happened to be born. Such a combination of art and celestial science affords perfect security of person, robust health and good fortune. What a handle to give any woman, but especially a superstitious one ! All the old threadbare arguments failing, an entirely new equipment is to be found in the astrology of Bond Street. The man who can stand up against the final home-thrust of his better and importunate half when couched in the language of the new cult of fashion, must have been born on a granite rock and fed on iron filings.

She.—" Dick, dear, I must have a new frock, a 'lucky colour' one, you know. They're all the fashion !"
He.—" Sorry, dearest ! Doesn't run to it. Awful bad luck lately, you know. Haven't found a winner this week !"
She.—" Well, how on earth can you expect to be lucky. Just look at that tie you're wearing. It's quite wrong for May. Really, it's positively courting bad luck to wear it !"

Of course he must have a new tie—the correct colour

for choice—and that means total and unconditional surrender, a visit to Regent Street under escort, and, of course, the coveted "Moon" robe and probably a "Venus" hat thrown in.

But underneath all this ephemeral and superficial study of planetary influence in daily life, there is a fundamental truth. A racing man told me the other day that the fascination of certain colours was irresistible. He had read up "form" until he was an embodiment of a Lunar Month, a Sporting Guide and a Turf Chronicle all in one. But he had only to go down to the course and get a glimpse of a "blue and white check," or a "black with red cap," and he was dished.

There may be a psychology attaching to the attraction certain colours have for us, and everybody has a taste of his own in this matter which cannot else be explained, but the man with a nose for problems will want to know what lies at the back of it. Do the planets have their corresponding colours, and are we influenced chiefly by those colours which are represented by planets figuring prominently in our respective horoscopes? When you come to carefully analyse the one hundred and one little things which go to make up your opinion about a person, you will find that colouring is not by any means an inconsiderable item in the equation. It may have been "those lips," or those auburn locks, or the clear depths of the blue eyes that looked in yours. But the chances are that the colour of the dress she wore had as much to do with it as anything else, and at the risk of appearing wholly unromantic I venture to say the wall-paper in the background of the picture played no unimportant part in the impression you took of her.

It is the same with sportsmen. The more I see of them the more fully do they confirm the general belief that they are, as a class, perhaps the most superstitious, and more influenced by what they call lucky omens, lucky numbers and lucky colours, than any other body of people to which my attention has been called. And if, as has been suggested, the planets dispose us in our likes and dislikes by the subtle influence of their rays at our nativities, it will be seen that a man has to be pretty high up in the scale of creation to be above it all.

But whether it be the folly of superstition or the instinctive recognition of a truth that makes us subservient to considerations of colour, in art as in nature, is a matter which may long remain problematical. It is, however, open to us to determine whether or not the predominance of a particular planet at the time of a race has any sort of connection or correspondence with the winning colours.

It has already been shown that apart from the natural fascination that colours exert upon the sense and mind, there may be some occult basis for the association of certain colours or combinations of colours with turf success. It has been suggested that if the planets have the influence in daily events of life which has been credited to them, it may be possible to find a line through their corresponding colours to the winner, a process which would apparently be more facile than tracing a line through a horse whose form is a variable quantity. That the planets exert an influence in our daily life may readily be argued from the scientific postulate of the solidarity of the solar system, for obviously the bodies of a system cannot act and react upon one another without mutually affecting the conditions of their respective inhabitants. For interplanetary action implies the transmission of energy which we recognise as Light, Force, Attraction, etc., and which affect the unstable equilibrium of the system and produce variations of the electrostatic condition of the earth's atmosphere, changes of weather, variations of wind, saturation and pressure. So that only if a man can claim to be independent of the very air he breathes can he logically assert indifference to planetary action. And this is putting the matter very crudely and superficially, for we do not yet know by what means differences of environment affect various individuals differently. But the action of the planets can be demonstrated experimentally in a variety of ways, and I am not begging the point in taking this as a fundamental proposition.

The planets are said to have a correspondence with colours, sounds, forms and numbers. We are now concerned with colours only. In the **Manual of Astrology** it will be found that the following colours correspond to the various planets.

NEPTUNE. Mauve, lavender, heliotrope, lilac.
SATURN. Black, dark blue, indigo, brown, and the darkest shades of all the colours.
URANUS. Checks, mixtures of black and white, grey, stripes and hoops, eccentricities, chevrons.
JUPITER. Violet, purple.
MARS. Red and scarlet.
VENUS. Pale blue, turquoise, and the art shades of blue and green.
MERCURY. Pink, dove and blue-grey.
MOON. White, silver, sea green, straw yellow.
SUN. Orange, gold.

The colours vary slightly from the primaries by planetary position and aspect, but the dominant colour of a planet should be conspicuous in the "winning colours" when that planet is a dominant factor in the horoscope of a race. That seems to be the logical outcome of this proposed association of planets and colours. Let us see how far it can be made to work.

The Lincoln Handicap horoscope shows Uranus in the 5th division of the heavens, which is held to rule speculative concerns. This planet indicates grey, or black and white hoops or stripes. Mr. F. S. Barnard's Kaffir Chief won and his jockey carried black and white hoops. The Liverpool Spring Cup won by St. Savin, owner Mr. Arthur James, colour lilac. Neptune was certainly not the strongest planet in the horoscope, but it occupied the sign of the Moon (Cancer) and the Moon was in the 5th house, which looks as if the Moon could borrow the colours of a planet in its sign. Worth noting.

Major Pennant's colours are not in the **Racing Handbook** for 1908, nor are those of Capt. C. P. B. Wood, so that I must pass over the Grand National and the Newbury Spring Cup. It is worth noting, however, in regard to "Rubio" (*Rubcus*=red) that the horoscope for the Grand National shows Mars (the red planet) in the mid-heaven joined to Venus in its own sign.

The Doveridge Handicap won by Altitude, owner Lord Derby, colours, black with white cap. The position of Uranus

Winning Colours

might indicate black and white, but the position of the Moon in its own sign along with Neptune would have favoured yellow or lilac, if represented. Saturn ruled the 5th house in this case and clearly shows "black"; but Mercury, who ruled both the mid-heaven and the ascendant of the horoscope, was setting in the sign Pisces and therefore too weak to assert its own colour. *Faute de mieux*, black won.

The Newark Plate won by Truffle de Perigord, owner Mr. G. Parrott, colours, cerise and white hoops, apple green collar, cuffs, and cap. Mercury rules the mid-heaven and ascendant and is conjoined with Saturn (ruling the 5th) which looks a good thing for "black," but both Saturn and Mercury are weak here. Mars and Venus are in the sign ruled by Mercury, which looks as though that planet had borrowed their colours.

Mr. J. Baird Thorneycroft's Damage won the Crawford Plate on April 22nd, colours, crimson, grey hoops and cap. The Moon was conjoined with Uranus, while Mars was in the sign of Mercury, who ruled the mid-heaven and ascendant, while Uranus ruled the 5th. Here we have the grey hoops of Uranus correctly indicated, and the crimson of Mars borrowed by Mercury.

The Jubilee Stakes won by Hayden, owner Mr. A. F. Bassett, colours, light blue and yellow hoops, scarlet sleeves and cap. The Moon ruled the mid-heaven, and Venus ruled the ascendant, while Uranus ruled the 5th house. The Moon shows yellow, Venus shows light blue, and Uranus denotes "hoops." The scarlet belongs to Mars, but it is difficult to bring it into the equation in this case as its influence is subsidiary to that of Mercury, who is not here the prime indicator of the colour.

Finally, Cargill won the Newmarket Handicap. It is owned by Lord Howard de Walden, whose colour is apricot. The Moon rules the mid-heaven, and Venus (in the Moon's sign) rules the ascendant. The Moon denotes yellow.

In sum it may be conceded that this matter of winning colours is worth a little study, and taken in connection with other indications from weight and number, may not be without its value in the problem of finding winners. I am chiefly concerned, however, to note that in effect it upholds the principles of astrology.

SYMBOLISM

Those who are interested in Symbolism will often catch a good thing in the wind without recourse to any calculation whatever. What, for instance, could be more patent than "White Knight" with the Moon rising in the sign Aries (ruled by Mars). Here the Moon is white and Mars the knight.

Royal Dream surely was a good tip with the Sun on the cusp of the 9th House, for all astrologers know that the Sun is king and that the 9th House is the House of dreams.

I have already mentioned "Rubio," the winner of the Grand National, and popularly known as "the milk-cart horse" who won at 66 to 1 against when Mars (*rubeus*=red) was on the mid-heaven. The student will, however, find that the weight of the horse answered to the gravity-point, and so there was no doubt about it whatever.

Signorinetta, who ran away with the Derby Stakes at 100 to 1 against in virtue of the Moon being the supreme planet in the heavens at the time, was another instance of cosmic symbolism difficult to avoid.

Cream of the Sky was a good name and an easy one to find in a race where the Moon was in its own sign Cancer and elevated in the horoscope.

These instances, taken from my notes on Symbolism, are quite convincing when taken with others too numerous to cite in this place. Those who are familiar with the language of the heavens will not fail to observe these sidelights. They are frequently very instructive.

THE LUNAR KEY

It is not enough that I have shown the merits and demerits of one or two methods which have been put forward with claims to the solving of the speculative problems, nor that I have said enough to safeguard the reader against the pitfalls which such systems inevitably lead to. Knowledge is, or ought to be, constructive, and in presenting the Lunar Key to the reader, I believe that I am giving him a certain means of unlocking more than one of the mysteries that surround the vexed question of successful speculation.

It has already been shown what great influence the Moon has in natural phenomena, and it has been stated that observation shows an extension of this influence beyond the inanimate world. It remains to demonstrate this, and show its application to the solution of problems which may truly be called speculative in the ordinary sense.

In a handicap race the competitors are distinguished by their weights. Handicapping presumes that the horses start as nearly as possible at equal terms, weight for age, plus penalty, being equivalent to handicapping by distance from scratch.

The difference between the highest and lowest weights carried by the competitors may, for convenience, be termed "the scale." Obviously, the acceptance weights must be taken, inasmuch as the heaviest weight to be carried will regulate the weights beneath it, so that it frequently happens that the weights assigned are raised on account of a top weight not accepting the impost. The acceptance weights being taken, the top and bottom weights represent the extremes of gravity which have to be overcome.

All that remains to be done is to find what weight the Moon's position corresponds with at the time of a race, for inasmuch as the Moon is a proved weight-lifter, we may naturally expect that gravity will be the more readily overcome in that instance, and that the performance of the animal carrying that weight will be proportionately good.

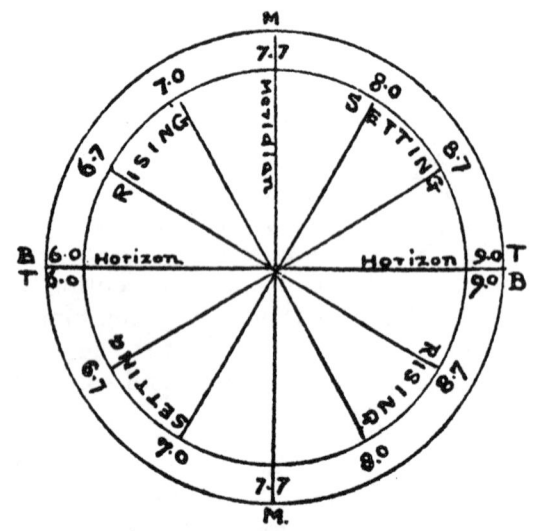

[diagram: circular chart divided into twelve segments showing weights at positions around a horoscope wheel. Labels include M 7.7, 7.0, 8.0, Rising, Setting, Meridian, 6.7, 8.7, B 6.0 / T 5.0 Horizon, Horizon 9.0 T / 9.0 B, Setting, Rising, 6.7, 8.7, 7.0, 8.0, 7.7 M.]

This problem may at first sight appear very difficult, but Uranus yields her secrets to the persistent and faithful suitor, and in event it was made clear to me that she is consistent with, and not contrary to, nature. Heavy things fall, and light things rise. Obviously, therefore, it is necessary to put the top weight on the West horizon where the planets set and the bottom weight on the East horizon where the planets rise. The mid-heaven, which is midway between the East and West horizons, will, therefore, denote the middle weight. Thus the whole range of weights will extend from the West to the East horizon.

Thus, if the top weight is 9st. and the bottom weight is 6st., the scale of 42 lbs. will be disposed as is shown on p. 76. [diagram above]

It will be seen that the weights corresponding with the

---

1 stone equals 14 pounds, or 6.35 kg. — *Publisher's note.*

horizon, namely T and B, amount in this instance to 15st., and similarly that the two weights, 8st. 7lbs., and 6st. 7lbs., at equal distances from the horizon amount to 15st., as do all others at equal distances from either T or B. The two weights are called "alternate" weights.

The Moon's position in regard to the horizon is constantly altering by the rotation of the Earth on its axis from West to East, so that in the course of about 12 hours the Moon appears to rise, culminate, and set.

At any point in time, therefore, it must be found somewhere between the points B M or M T if above the horizon, or between the points T M or M B if below the horizon.

It will, therefore, be necessary to find the Moon's place at any time in reference to the horizon of any locality.

HOW TO SET THE FIGURE

In the Table of Sidereal Times find the sidereal time corresponding with the required date.

To this sidereal time *add* the time p.m. at which the event takes place.

Next refer to the Table of Ascensions under the nearest latitude, and find the ascendant corresponding to the time obtained by the preceding rule.

Having noted this ascendant, which is the point of the zodiac rising at the time of the event, you must now refer to an ephemeris for the Moon's place at noon on the given date.

An ephemeris is an astronomical journal in which the place of the Sun, Moon, and planets is given for each day of the year at noon. The motion of the Moon varies from day to day, and from hour to hour, but the mean motion of 13° 11' (nearly) may be taken as the basis of the calculation for the hourly increment, so that if we take 1° 6' for every two hours, or 33' for an hour, or 16' for half-an-hour, and *add* this to the longitude at noon, as shown in the ephemeris, we shall be quite within the limits required for our purpose.

Example.—Required the Moon's place for 3 p.m., March 21st, 1911.

The ephemeris shows the Moon at noon in 13° 17' of Sagittarius.

Then longitude	♐ 13° 17'
Plus motion for 3h. p.m....	1° 30'
Approximate long. Moon	14° 47'

How to Set the Figure

Now to find the Moon's distance in longitude from the horizon :—

	H.	M.
Sidereal Time for March 21st	23	52
Time p.m...	3	0
	26	52
Subtract the circle...	—24	0
Refer to ascendant under	2	52

This sidereal time must now be looked for under the latitude nearest the locality of the race meeting. Let us suppose Newmarket. The Table for Birmingham, Leicester, Warwick, Newmarket, Wolverhampton, etc., is referred to, and we find the nearest to 2h. 52m. is either 2h. 50m. or 2h. 54m. In such case we take the later time as more likely to coincide with the event. Against 2h. 54m. we find the ascendant to be ♌ 28°, *i.e.*, 28° of the sign Leo.

This means that the 28° of Leo is rising at Newmarket at 3 p.m. on March 21st, 1911, and consequently the *same degree* of the *opposite sign*, Aquarius ♒, is setting.

The Moon, which was found to be in ♐ 14° 47' will, therefore, be 73° below the West horizon, and this is the point of gravity. The Moon's direct line of lifting power is exerted from a point 73° below the West horizon to a point 73° above the East horizon, and the weight falling *on or nearest* to this line of gravity must be noted.

SIGNS OF THE ZODIAC, WITH THEIR SYMBOLS, WHICH ARE OPPOSED.

Aries	..	..	♈	Libra	..	..	♎
Taurus	..	..	♉	Scorpio	..	..	♏
Gemini	..	..	♊	Sagittarius	..	..	♐
Cancer	..	..	♋	Capricornus	..	..	♑
Leo	..	..	♌	Aquarius	..	..	♒
Virgo	..	..	♍	Pisces	..	..	♓

Each sign of the zodiac includes 30° of the zodiac.

The Tables of Sidereal Time and those of the Ascendants will be found at the end of this book.

Note.—For convenience of working, anything over 30" is counted as 1' and anything over 30' is counted as 1°. When below 30 they may be rejected.

ELONGATION OF MOON

It has already been stated that the whole effect of the tides is not due to the Moon, but some share of it is due to the Sun, and their combined attraction exerted from different parts of the heavens, and in different directions, determines the magnitude and the time of the tide.

Research has shown similarly that the Moon's distance from the Sun (called elongation) has a value scarcely less than the Moon itself, for it will be found that a point at the same distance from the horizon as the Moon is distant from the Sun, will exert an influence as great as if the Moon itself was there. As the Moon increases or diminishes its distance from the Sun this point increases or diminishes its distance from the horizon, so that, as the combined motions of Sun and Moon result in a mean increase of elongation amounting to about 12° per day, the gravity point in relation to the horizon will progress at an average rate of 12° per day through the zodiac. Call this point G. In the example already given for 3 p.m., March 21st, 1911, the Moon was found in ♐ 15°, and the Sun on that day is in ♓ 30°, so that the point G will be 75° from the horizon, that being the number of degrees between the Moon and Sun.

Note.—At new and full Moon the point G will be on the horizon; at 1st and 3rd quarters of the Moon it will be 90° from the horizon, and therefore on the meridian. The nearest distance between the Sun and Moon is always to be taken, and when it exceeds 90° take it from 180° to obtain the point G. We have now two points, that of the Moon's distance above the horizon, and that of the point G. These are found to be 14° and 18° from the horizon respectively. The weights corresponding with these points, and the complemental weights corresponding with their opposite points, will answer

Elongation of Moon

to the winner in such a large percentage of cases as to place the matter entirely beyond all shadow of doubt.

THE TEST

Now let us see how the theory works out in practice. For this purpose I will take a record from the calendar of 1910, beginning at Warwick on September 12th.

On this day there were handicaps at 3.0 and 4:30 p.m.

Warwick, September 12th, 1910.

	H. M.
Sidereal time at noon	11 22
Subtract for Warwick, west long.	—6
	11 16
Time p.m.	3 0
	14 16

The ascendant answering to this is ♑ 0°. The Moon's longitude was ♐ 28°, and that of the Sun ♍ 19°, the Moon's elongation being therefore 81°. Thus from ♍ 19° to ♐ 28° is 99°, and this, as it exceeds 90°, when taken from 180° leaves 81°, which is the distance from the West horizon of point G.

The Moon is in ♐ 28°, and the ascendant in ♑ 0°, so that the Moon is just 2° above the horizon. The figure therefore stands as follows:

☾ ♐ 28°		
♑ 0°	81° G	♋ 0°

Now it has already been stated that the "scale" of weights extends from the West to the East horizon and back again. Consequently the Moon, which is close to the horizon, will

The Test

indicate the top and bottom weights as in the line of its gravity, while G being near the meridian will denote a weight close to the middle of the scale of weights. The acceptances were :

T 8 st. 1 lb. ———— 7 st. 3 lbs. B.

The difference between the top and bottom weights is therefore 12 lbs. Half of this is 6 lbs., and the middle weight is therefore 7 st. 9 lbs. This weight was carried by Scarlet Runner, who won at 100 to 7; and Donnez-moi who carried 7 st. 8 lbs., was third

Warwick, 4.30 p.m.

	H.	M.
Sidereal time for September 12th, at 3 p.m.	14	16
Add for time elapsed	1	30
	15	46

This answers to the ascendant in ♑24°. The ☽ is in ♐ 28° as before, and the ☉ in ♍ 19°—G=81° as before.

The weights involved were:

	ST.	LBS.
Top	8	7
Bottom	—7	0
Difference	1st	7lbs = 21 lbs.

Then as 21 lbs. extends over 180°, the scale for 90° will be 10½ lbs. The Moon's distance from horizon is 26°. Hence the proportion

as 90° is to 10½ lbs. so is 26°

which gives 3 lbs. This amount taken from the top, and added to the bottom weight, yields 8 st. 4 lbs. and 7 st. 3 lbs. as the two weights which fall in the direct line of the Moon's gravity. The nearest to 8 st. 4 lbs. was the top weight, which did not show up at all. The nearest to 7 st. 3 lbs. was 7 st. 2 lbs., Tipperary Lass, who ran in third. It will be noted that 7 st. 3 lbs. is the weight corresponding with the Moon's place, while 8 st. 4 lbs. is its opposite or complemental weight.

Now let us look at the point of horizontal gravity G. This is at 81°, answering to the Moon's elongation; then—

The Silver Key

as 90° : 10½ lbs. :: 81° : 9½ lbs.

This quantity applied to the top and bottom weights in the scale, gives

7 st. 11½ lbs. and 7 st. 9½ lbs.

The nearest to both these weights was 7 st. 9 lbs., Claret Lad, who won at evens.

At the same place next day, September 13th, 1910, we have handicaps at 2.0, 2:30, 3:30, and 4 o'clock.

	H.	M.
The Sidereal time for Sept. 13th is 11 h. 26 m. less 6 mins. for West longitude of Warwick = ...	11	20
Add time p.m.	2	0
Sidereal time at 2 p.m...	13	20
		30
Sidereal time at 2:30 p.m.	13	50
	1	0
Sidereal time at 3:30 p.m.	14	50
		30
Sidereal time at 4.0 p.m...	15	20

The ascendants answering to these amounts are ♐ 17°, ♐ 24°, ♑ 8° and ♑ 16°.

The Sun's longitude is ♍ 20°, and the Moon at noon is in ♑ 8° 23'; then

At 2.0 the ☽ is in ♑ 9°
At 2:30 " " 10
At 3:30 " " 10
At 4.0 " " 10

The Moon's elongation is 71° at 2 o'clock, and 70° thereafter.

Let us see what results we can get from these figures:

2.0.—The nearest to 9 st. 7 lbs. was Tokay, who carried 9 st. 9 lbs., and ran third. None of the other weights

The Test

showed up. The race was won by Rapt, whose acceptance weight was 8 st. 1lb.

2:30.—This was won by Syce with 8 st. 9 lbs. in the saddle.

3:30.—G gives the winner in Paulhan, who carried 8 st. 9 lbs., and was priced at 10 to 1.

4.0.—G again gives the winner in Orchestrelle, who carried 11 st. 9 lbs., the nearest to 11 st. 11 lb. Starting price 13 to 8.

It will be shown later how to distinguish between M and G, and why on this occasion G would have been followed throughout the day. In effect we have the following result.

We can now tabulate these particulars, together with the weights involved in each event, see below.

The first column contains the schedule time of the race and corresponding ascendant.

The second column shows the distances of the Moon and point G from the horizon.

The third column contains the acceptance weights remaining in on the day of the event.

		Scale of Weights	Gravity Weights
2.0	M 22	9.10 — 8.0	M 9.7 — 8.3
♐ 17	G 71		G 9.0 — 8.10
2:30	M 16	9.3 — 6.10	M 9.0 — 6.13
♐ 24	G 70		G 8.3 — 7.10
3:30	M 2	9.0 — 7.12	M 9.0 — 7.12
♑ 8	G 70		G 8.8 — 8.4
4.0	M 6	12.9 — 10.7	M 12.8 — 10.8
♑ 16	G 70		G 11.11 — 11.5

The Silver Key

The last column contains the gravity weights and the weights corresponding to the distances in column two.

Warwick, September 12th, 1910.

	st.	lbs.			
3.0 ..	7	9	Scarlet Runner	..	.. Won 100/7
	7	8	Donnez-moi	..	.. Third
4:30 ..	7	12	Claret Lad ⎫	..	.. Won evens
	7	9	Ditto ⎭		

Warwick, September 13th, 1910.

	st.	lbs.			
2.0 ..	9	0	Dandalloo	..	.. Lost
	8	10	Grey Parrot	..	.. "
2:30 ..	8	3	Retrenchment	..	.. Third
	7	10	The Best	..	.. Lost
3:30 ..	8	8	Paulhan	..	.. Won 10/1
	8	4	Princess Queen	..	.. Lost
4.0 ..	11	11	Orchestrelle	..	.. Won 13/8
	11	5	Gorgophone	..	.. Second

On balance we have won .. .. 27 points
Lost .. .. −7 "

Leaving a net gain of .. .. 20 "

On September 14th there was racing at Yarmouth and Ayr. Yarmouth is 6 m. east of Greenwich, and Ayr is 18 m. west of Greenwich.

Yarmouth, September 14th, 1910.

	H.	M.
Sidereal time for this date	11	30
Plus for E. long.		6
Sidereal time for Yarmouth ..	11	36
Time p.m.	2	0
	13	36
Add for 3 p.m.	1	0
	14	36

Moon in ♑22°, elongation 59°, Sun in ♍21°.

The Test

		Scale of Weights	Gravity Weights
2.0 ♐21	M 31 G 59	9.2 — 7.7	M 8.12 — 7.11 G 8.9 — 8.0
3.0 ♑4	M 18 G 59	8.12 — 6.5	M 8.9 — 6.8 G 8.1 — 7.2

The winner at 2.0 was Jinks' gelding, who carried 8 st. 7 lb. There were three runners at 8 st. 9 lb.

At 3.0 the Norfolk and Suffolk Handicap was won by St. Mac, the nearest to G 7st. 2 lb., who started at 10 to 1. Yarmouth therefore yields 7 points net gain.

Ayr, September 14th, 1910.

	H.	M.
Sidereal time for Sept. 14	11	30
Less per W. longitude	—	18
Sidereal time for Ayr at noon..	11	12
Add time p.m.	1	45
Ascendant in ♐ 9°	12	57
Add for 2:15 p.m.		30
Ascendant in ♐ 15°	13	27
Add for 5:15 p.m.	3	0
Ascendant in ♒ 2°	16	27

Sun in ♍ 20°

Moon at 1:45 in ♑ 22°, elongation= 58
" 2:15 " 22 " 58
" 5:15 " 24 " 56

The Silver Key

		Scale of Weights	Gravity Weights
1:45 ✗9	M 43 G 58	9.0 — 7.10	M 8.10 — 8.0 G 8.8 — 8.2
2:15 ✗15	M 37 G 58	12.10 — 10.0	M 12.2 — 10.8 G 11.12 — 10.12
5:15 ♒2	M 10 G 56	9.0 — 6.7	M 8.12 — 6.9 G 8.3 — 7.4

    1:45 was won by Killiecrankie, 7 st. 13 lbs., being the nearest to M 8 st. as required by the Rule of Selection (which see).

    2:15 was won by King's Proctor under G 11 st. 12 lb.

    5:15 was won by "S.S.," 7 st. 3 lb., under G 7 st. 4 lb.

    The results therefore yield:

1:45	Neidr, 8 st. 11 lb.	.. .. Lost
	Killiecrankie, 7 st. 13 lb.	.. .. .. Won 100/8
2:15	King's Proctor, 11 st. 11 lb.	.. .. " 5/2
	Salomet, 10 st. 12 lb.	.. .. .. Lost
5:15	Nil	.. .. *
	S.S., 7 st. 3 lb.	.. .. Won 3/1

    * The nearest weight to 8 st. 3 lb. among the runners was 7 st. 6 lb., which is too far removed from the point of gravity to be admitted. A ninth part of the scale is quite enough to allow in any case.

    Ayr therefore yields 16 points net gain on this day, and Yarmouth 7 points, making 23 points net gain.

    On September 16th there was racing at Ayr, Manchester, and Hurst Park.

    Ayr.—The 2:45, 3:20, and 4.0 races gave a net result of 5 points gain.

    Manchester.—The 3.0, 3:30, and 4:30 handicaps brought in a net gain of 8 points.

The Test

Hurst Park.—The 3.0, 4.0, and 4:30 race yielded a gain of 16½ points, making a total on the day of 29½ points.

On the 17th at Hurst Park the 2:30, 3.0, 4.0, and 4:30 handicaps brought in 7 points gain. At Manchester on the same day the 2:15, 3.0, and 3:30 were all won by the indicated weights and yielded a net gain of 8 points, making the total for the day 15 points gained.

In order that the reader may check these figures, I append a correct acceptance list of scales of weights on September 16th and 17th for the events referred to at the various places. I want nothing to be taken for granted.

Ayr, September 16th—

	T st. lb.	B st. lb.	Gravity Point
2:45	9 10	6 7	G
3:20	12 7	10 0	G
4.0	9 0	7 3	G

Manchester—

3.0	9 0	6 0	M
3:30	9 0	7 7	G
4:30	9 3	7 0	G

Hurst Park—

3.0	9 0	6 9	M
4.0	9 0	6 12	M
4:30	10 0	7 0	G

Hurst Park, September 17th—

2:30	9 0	7 0	M
3.0	9 0	6 0	M
4.0	9 0	7 0	M
4:30	9 7	6 7	M

Manchester—

2:15	9 4	6 5	M
3.0	9 0	6 0	M
3:30	9 5	7 10	M

As back numbers of the Calendar are difficult to obtain, and the acceptances are not given in the racing returns, the above list will enable anyone to make the calculations with the aid of an ephemeris for 1910. An ephemeris for any

The Silver Key

year since 1800 can be obtained for the sum of one shilling. The best is that published by Raphael. Raphael's shilling almanac now contains both an ephemeris and an aspectarian, and on this account may be preferred.

The following are the results of the working of this method from September 20th to the end of the month :—

September 20th	— net gain —	13 points
"	21st	"	3	"
"	22nd	"	13	"
"	23rd	lost	2	"
"	24th	net gain	14½	"
"	27th	"	2	"
"	28th	"	8	"
"	29th	lost	5	"
"	30th	net gain	12	"

In nine days the total net gain is thus 65½ points, which, added to 87½ points gained from the 12th to 17th inclusive, yields 153 points gained in 15 days, an average of 10 points per day.

It will be seen that the method entails a probability of one of two weights being that nearest to the weight carried by the winner, and hence it is necessary to place a stake on each of them. But inasmuch as anything over evens will yield a gain, a method which gives 60 per cent. of winning events, many of them at long odds, must obviously be worth following.

The method has, moreover, the following singular advantages over any scientific method hitherto employed. It does not require that the "off" time of an event be known. It is entirely free from the ambiguity of "coding," or estimating the value of a horse's name. It makes no consideration of jockeyship, ownership or form. It ignores all tips. The whole of the calculations for one day can be made in a few minutes. The full acceptance weights of the competitors left in on the day are employed, and, therefore, all that is required is to find the two horses carrying the nearest weights to those indicated. One is generally a well-tipped horse or a favourite, and the other an outsider. The latter wins as often as not.

Having now displayed the method of calculating the points of gravity, and the corresponding weights, it remains only to discern between the points M and G. This will now be done.

POLARITY

If we take a bar of iron, or any other magnetic agent, and pass a current of electricity through its length, we have a polarised body, the molecules of which have undergone a change. We may disturb this molecular arrangement by heating the iron, and so destroy its magnetic property. But while it is polarised from end to end it is also affected by transverse magnetism at right angles to the line of its polarity. Thus a magnetic needle will always turn at right angles to a superposed current of electricity.

Now in every locality there are two planes or circles, which are found to be capable of excitation by planetary action. These are the meridian circle and the horizontal circle, and they are at right angles to one another. If a planet is found on the mid-heaven, and therefore in coincidence with the meridian circle, it is found that it not only affects that circle but simultaneously the circle of the horizon also.

Hence when the Moon is on the mid-heaven, it sometimes brings in T or B, and the middle weight indicated by the mid-heaven does not show up. Similarly, when the Moon is on the horizon it may on occasions bring in the middle weight, although its direct indication would be top or bottom weight.

The matter would seem to depend on the coincidence of certain other factors, such as a planet rising or setting at the time, or in square aspect to the ascendant. But the introduction of these factors would only tend to complicate what otherwise must be regarded as an extremely simple, and at the same time satisfactory approach to a solution of the speculative problem, and I propose, therefore, to leave the matter where it is for the present. I may say this much, however, without in any way perplexing the reader, when the Moon is at or near the quadrature, *i.e.*, 90° from the Sun, and at the same time just about rising or setting, the *middle weight* will win.

Of course, every body in the solar system exerts some attraction on the Earth, and a full computation of all these forces, taking the masses and distances of the several bodies into consideration, would give us a greater frequency of successful results; but the equation is quite beyond the powers of the average reader, and it will, therefore, doubtless content him to know that the Moon is, in proportion to its mass, so powerful in its action on the Earth as to outweigh the attraction of any other body in the system, so far as sensible effects enable us to discern.

SELECTION

If it were required by any system that as many as four indicated competitors have a winning chance, that system would need to be screened. Having found that either M or G will yield the correct result in over 75 per cent. of cases, the next step was, of course, to determine which of the two indicators gave the greater number of correct results, or rather, which of them was the more frequently employed. A scrutiny of a large number of consecutive cases showed that there was most frequently a run on one of them, followed by a run on the other, and in effect, both were equally employed, but sporadically.

An attempt was then made to discover the law underlying this alternation, and although it cannot be claimed that any definite conclusion was arrived at, it was found that by employing a simple factor, the greater number of indicated results could be secured. In short a method of selection was discovered, which I may now proceed to explain.

In astrological experience it has transpired that planetary bodies act upon us at certain angles, that is to say, their rays affect us only when transmitted at definite angular distances, while at others they produce no appreciable effect whatever. These angles are called "aspects," and it has been found that they correspond to the angles, or complemental angles, of a regular polygon inscribed within a circle, and are identical with the angles at which water and the "superior metals" crystallise.

THE ASPECTS

These aspects are (beside the position called conjunction), 15°, 30°, 45°, 60°, 72°, 90°, 120°, 135°, and 180°.

There are 30° in each sign of the zodiac, and, therefore, the distance of one body from another can easily be ascertained. Thus two positions or bodies holding the same degree of different signs will be *in aspect* to one another.

If in adjacent signs they will be 30° apart. If one sign intervenes they will be 60° apart. If two signs intervene they will be 90° apart. One and a half signs is an aspect of 45°, as when a planet is in the beginning of one sign and another in the middle of the next sign; or, one in the middle of a sign and another at the end of the following sign. Two signs and 12°, make an angle or "aspect" of 72°. It is one-fifth of the circle.

Thus 360° ÷ 2 = 180°, the opposition aspect.
" 360° ÷ 3 = 120°, the trine aspect.
" 360° ÷ 4 = 90°, the square aspect.
" 360° ÷ 5 = 72°, the quintile aspect.
" 360° ÷ 6 = 60°, the sextile aspect.
" 360° ÷ 8 = 45°, the semi-square aspect.
" 360° ÷ 10 = 36°, the semi-quintile or decile aspect.
" 360° ÷ 12 = 30°, the semi-sextile aspect.

Those which are operative in the present case are the following :— 90°, 72°, 60°, 45°, and 30°, as well as the conjunction.

Applying this information to the problem of selection, it is only necessary to note whether M or G is nearest in any aspect to the horizon, i.e., to the degree of the zodiac which is on the East or West horizon. Whichever may thus be in most complete aspect to the horizon must be taken as the

The Aspects

indicator, and the weights corresponding to its position must be regarded as having the major operative influence.

Noted that an indicator that is more than 3° from the true aspect is not effective.

If both M and G are inoperative on account of being out of aspect with the horizon, then M is generally to be preferred.

Similarly when both M and G are at equal distances from a complete aspect, M is to be preferred.

Thus, M 32° from the horizon and G 46° from the horizon, G is to be preferred, because it is only 1° from the 45° aspect, whereas the Moon (M) is 2° from the 30° aspect, and G is therefore in closer aspect to the horizon.

M at 56° and G at 64°, both are at the same distance from the complete 60° aspect, and hence M is to be preferred, unless, as may be the case, G is going from 64° to 63° in its course, while M is going from 54 to 53°. In this case G is applying to the 60° aspect and every minute will bring it nearer, while M is separating from the 60°, and is losing its aspect, and therefore its influence.

These principles being duly noted and carefully applied nothing hinders that the practical student should turn this information to his advantage, as assuredly he will if he first of all convinces himself by experiment of its truth, and afterwards applies it to the problems in hand with dispassionate impartiality.

An alternative method to the above, which has suggested itself to my mind, is as follows:

Take the proportional distance of the Moon from the horizon, instead of its actual distance in longitude. Thus if 17° Pisces is on the meridian of London, then 18° Cancer will be rising, and the quadrant from the meridian to the horizon eastward will include 121° of the zodiac.

Now suppose that the Moon is in 7° Taurus, it will then be 71° from the horizon by longitude. Thus to get its proportional distance say:

The Silver Key

As 121° of the zodiac
is to 90° of the quadrant,
so is 71° of the zodiac

to $\dfrac{71 \times 90}{121}$ =53 nearly.

The Moon's proper distance from the horizon is therefore 53°, and its proportional distance from the meridian will be 37°, which is the complement required to make 90°.

This suggestion is not intended to replace a well-tried method, but is merely offered as a ground for possible research work, and I am aware that the complemental arc will generally fit the case where the horizontal has failed. But inasmuch as the majority of results must control our judgment in speculative matters, I have no hesitation in offering the "Silver Key" method as the best solution of the problem of speculative values.

FAVOURITES

The public will generally be on the right track when at the time of an event the Moon is separating from a complete aspect of Neptune, Uranus, Saturn or Mars, and applying to an aspect with Jupiter, Venus, Sun or Mercury, and more particularly when the aspect the Moon is about to form is a good one, *i.e.*, 60°, 120°, or a conjunction with Jupiter or Venus.

GRAVITY AND EVOLUTION

In connection with this interesting question of the attraction of gravitation, to which science has given a name, but about which we understand very little beyond the observed effects, it may be of some instruction to notice how, in response to a certain upward pull exerted by nature on the minds of men, humanity has gradually overcome this attraction of gravitation which binds man to his mother Earth. In the very early days of artificial locomotion men used sleighs, either drawn by hand or by beasts, and great weights could not very easily be dealt with on this account. Then some genius invented wheels, and bullock and horse-drawn vehicles came into general use. From the point of view of gravity, the stage-coach may be regarded as the most effective of these structures until we come to new methods of propulsion by steam, petrol and electricity. Meanwhile a development was taking place in aquatic locomotion, by which gravity was increasingly overcome until we reached the swift-going turbine. The iron road was a further development of this effort to overcome gravity, and the evolution of the steam locomotive travelling at sixty miles an hour brought about the realisation of Sir Isaac Newton's prophecy that in order to fulfil certain prophecies in the Bible it would be necessary that men should travel at the rate of sixty miles an hour !

Having displaced to a very appreciable extent the attraction of gravitation exerted by the earth on land and sea, man next set about the problem of complete detachment which had to some extent been solved by aeronautics. Balloons had risen to great heights and had been carried by the winds at great velocities in uncertain directions. Further detachment could be effected by control of direction, and in due course the dirigible balloon came into existence, and last of all the aeroplane, which gave not only power of elevation but also power of direction. Thus man, answering to the upward pull by which his evolution is effected, has gradually asserted dominion over land and water and air. The day is bound to come when he will understand and utilise the great etheric currents which play about the globe on which he lives. He will then know that the Moon and Sun alone do not produce tides on the earth, but that there are etheric tides caused by the relative positions of the planets in regard to any locality, and he will then not only see the cause of atmospheric disturbances but will also be well assured of the fact of planetary influence in human life.

A CALCULATOR

For Finding The Distances Of Celestial Bodies From The Horizon In Longitude.

In order to facilitate the calculation of the Moon's distances from the horizon, I have invented a little astrolabe which shows the position of the Moon in relation to the horizon at any point of time, together with the aspect it throws to the ascending degree.

Having the sidereal time at noon on any date, the time p.m. must be added, or, if a.m., the time before noon must be subtracted, and with the resulting amount reference is made to the Table of Ascendants, and the longitude against the sidereal time is then brought to the point marked "Ascdt. 0" in the Calculator. Then by reference to the Ephemeris of the year current, it will be seen in what longitude the Moon is on the given date. This being noted on the revolving dial, its distance from the horizon will be seen in the marginal circle.

The inside or revolving circle contains the signs of the zodiac divided into intervals of 5°. This circle can be revolved in either direction by merely pushing the stud at ♈ one way or the other.

The outside or fixed circle represents the prime vertical, or that circle in which the observer stands upright. On the left is the ascendant, on the right the descendant, above is the M.C. (Medium Coeli) or midheaven, and below is the nadir, marked I.C. (Imaum Coeli), or lowest point in the heavens. At proportionate distances from the horizon, in either direction, the aspects are marked in degrees; so that the Moon's aspect to the horizon may be known by inspection,

A Calculator

and the point G is always the same distance from the horizon as the Moon is from the Sun or its opposition, whichever may be nearest.

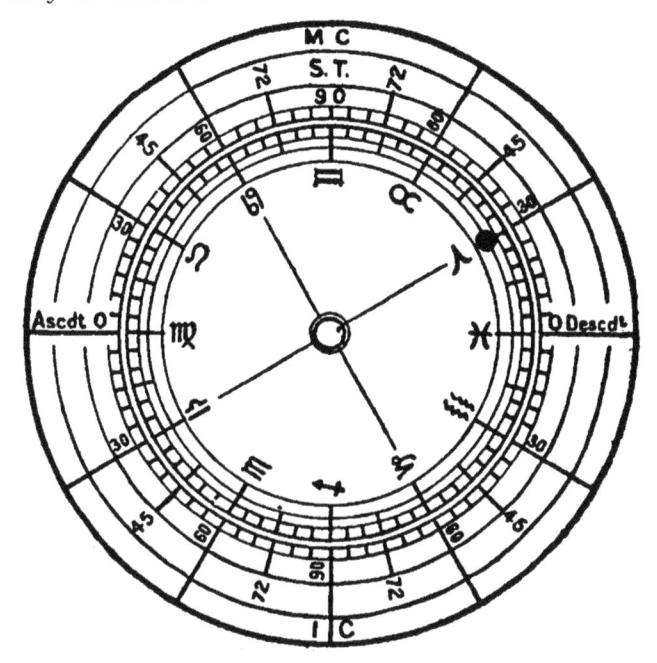

Thus on March 28th, 1911, at 3:20 p.m., the observation is as follows:—

	H.	M.	S.
Sidereal time at noon ..	0	19	8
Time p.m. add	3	20	0
	3	39	8

which, referred to the Table of Ascendants, gives −6° on the E. horizon. I turn the revolving dial until −6° is on the line marked "Ascdt 0," and a glance at the Ephemeris shows that the Moon is in ♈10° 31' at noon, to which 1° 40' being added for 3:20 p.m. gives ♈12° 11', as the approximate longitude of the Moon. Its place on the dial shows that it is 6° from the West horizon.

Then for the point G.

Sun's longitude	♈ 7°	
Moon's do.	♓ 12°	
From ☽ to end of ♓		= 18°
From end of ♓ to ♈ 7°		= 7°
		25°

The point G is therefore at 25° above the E horizon, as the Moon is going to a conjunction with the Sun.

SOMETHING TO COME

Your average experience will include this phrase as among the sweetest sounding expressions of turf parlance. You have backed a winner or two in the course of the week, you have "gone down" on one or two, but on balance there is "something to come," and that after all is what interest in racing or any other form of speculation amounts to when it is a constant quantity. Something to come is what Nature offers us for all the effort we put forth for the benefit of other, and not more than this can the best of us hope for when the account is made up. The sportsman would be a poor fellow indeed if he had not a live interest in his pastime. For powder and shot he expects his bag, or at least better sport to-morrow, and for that to-morrow he is qualifying by every deliberate shot he makes to-day. It is the same with horse-racing. Every failure means success, if only you are in earnest. The man who backs his fancy without anything to show for it, is like one firing a blunderbuss at random in a covert. He may be lucky enough to bring something down, if it's only a man ! But that is not sport, or nobody would think of it in the same category with big game hunting or deer-stalking, though of course it is all "shooting" of a sort.

I have great respect for the man who makes a close study of "form," who makes a patient study of the performances of the various candidates in a big event, following his lines through until they lead him to the winner. It is work which requires patience, a good memory, accurate observation and no little judgment. But I have even more respect for one who recognises the inconstancy of form and tries to find the hidden law which apparently lies at the back of the changes taking place in the kaleidoscope. He may begin with the law of averages, may go on to consider the law of permutations, and inevitably will end in something like a settled belief in the virtue and power of Numbers, of Sound and Colour, and planetary influence. Not that, even with the most perfect key, one may not fail at times to unlock the door.

But with such a key in hand the chances of success are immeasurably increased. Let the matter rest there for awhile. There are other matters to consider.

A WARNING

I am quite in agreement with a writer of **The Referee** who declared that the abuse of the sporting press by professional tipsters is the chief cause of the odium attaching to it. The man who is not a regular follower of turf matters cannot or does not discriminate. When he sees the advertisements of these men in the papers after every big event claiming to have given the winner by "special" or "discretionary" wires or other means of securing a faked result in their favour, he is induced to try his luck. It is not long before his eyes are open to the methods of "plotting," "farming," "homing," etc., pursued by the tipster, whose sole work in the world is to relieve fools of their superfluous cash.

"Plotting" consists in working various plots or areas with startling advertisements. In any big event the four or five horses likely to win are sent on as many separate wires to four or five sporting papers as "vouchers."

One of the papers gets the winner and this is worked for all it is worth by large advertisements in the next and subsequent issues. Of the other four nothing more is heard for a time, but their turns are bound to come, and there is plenty of scope for operations.

"Farming" is a term applied by professional tipsters to the method alluded to by the writer in **The Referee**. The selections of the various papers are sent out in batches, so there is always a certain number on the list of subscribers who get the right wire, and if the others complain they are told that only the "late" wires or the "special" wires, or some other description of wires got the correct thing referred to in the advertisement; and before a man can catch these rogues tripping, he has to get *all* their wires for the same event sent to him under different names and to different addresses. Then he knows as much as I can tell him and will have paid about as much for his experience. But you cannot get legislation to do this sort of thing, and that is why, if you please, they want to bring in a bill to prevent a man putting even a shilling on his own selection ! The "homers" rely for their success on a number of testimonials which they send to one another for publication, "references given" in fact, which in effect is nothing less than nefarious log-rolling.

ON SPECULATION

Speculation appears to be a radical component of human nature. From the "casting lots" of ancient days to modern "punting" is a direct and continuous line of the exercise of this ineradicable trait of character. When the son of Virasena gambled away his kingdom in the days of the Mâhâbhârat, he was actuated by the same spirit of speculation that induces the man in the street to put his last half-crown upon the special "Nap" of an irresponsible journalist.

In the good days to come we shall do our racing for its own sake—to the village pump and back, so to speak—in the old-fashioned way. Privileged owners and members of the Jockey Club will doubtless be allowed to pool the stakes and in all probability they, under the espionage of certain representatives of the Anti-Gambling League, will have the field to themselves. Is it to be expected that Tom, Dick, and Harry will pay ten shillings, or even half-a-crown, to watch other men winning money without a chance of getting a little side sport of the same kind?

But who invented the statement that gambling was a modern craze? Canon Horsley knows his Scripture well enough to recollect that Jacob refused a wage of Laban and preferred a flutter on the "streaked lambs." This would have been a fair sporting chance had not the future patriarch known a thing or two more about sheep-farming than old Laban.

Pooling results, drawing and casting lots, wages and sweepstakes are among the most ancient forms of human polity. Oriental literature, both sacred and profane, is full of it. It may be an evil, like everything else, by abuse. But a man to be a responsible agent must be a free agent, and accountable to himself in this as in other matters. For if he can acquit himself of no undue extravagance, or trespass upon his neighbour's rights, there will be found none to upbraid him. And after everything has been said upon the subject, it will puzzle the most ardent member of the Anti-Gambling League to name a single enterprise, industry, investment, or financial interest whatsoever, which is not *au fond* as much a speculation as the biggest wild-cat scheme that was ever subscribed by the Clergy List. The whole of life is a speculation to the man who does not know.

Any true lover of horses cannot fail to be interested in breeding and performance, and beyond that the question remains as to whether merits and reward should not continue to be closely related in this matter as in all other kinds of human interest, and in such case, whether it is derogatory to the individual or detrimental to the public morals for sportsmen to have a live interest in the achievements of equine heroes? Beyond that lies the greater question which well deserves the consideration of the British Slave, namely, whether a man, being honestly possessed of certain spare money cannot dispose of it as he wishes, provided that in so doing he does not offend against the rights of his neighbour? Necessarily any course of action which tends to the detriment of the individual has its reaction on society at large, and for this reason it is well to have laws which guide and direct the course of individual life, but any law which limits and curtails the freedom of the well-disposed citizen is a barrier to progress.

Consequently, in the fuller and more perfect realisation of individual responsibility, which will eventually arise from the liberality of public education and opinion, we may be prepared to find a more generous legislation on all matters affecting public sports and pastimes, and in course of time laws may be enacted which will recognise the private interest equally with the stakes of the Jockey Club and provide for its protection. As between the suppression of all forms of public speculation and the liberty of the subject, the latter must ever be paramount in the minds of astute legislators, and the futility of trying to elicit a greater sense of personal responsibility by the legal suppression and curtailment of natural inclinations must be evident to every trained mind. There is no curriculum for the making of saints, but possibly

On Speculation

there is a stage in the evolution of the man where betting and speculation are left behind. It is safe to say that many of our lawmakers have been successful gamblers, and the average man wants also his measure of success, and freedom to enjoy it without vexatious intermeddling on the part of spontaneous and prejudiced reformers.

It has been said that in order to make speculation a success, one must have a fortunate horoscope, that is, fortunate for speculation. One does not, however, need this "lucky star" in order to wrest favours from Dame Fortune. This fickle jade trades upon the credulity of the ignorant, but is found to be obedient enough to those who know enough of the "law" to put a check upon her vagaries. We only speak of "luck" and "chance" when we would avoid a confession of our own ignorance of the law underlying the correlated successiveness of events. It is a bad habit, borrowed from quasi-scientific men who stick a label on a thing to obscure their ignorance and to avoid discussion. Before Newton's time things fell to the earth by their weight, and because they were heavier than air. Hydrogen rises, carrying a man with it perchance, merely because it is lighter than air. But since Newton's day these things have answered to the name of Gravity, and so we call them. But what the attraction of gravitation may be, whereby bodies are urged to a common centre and planets are kept in their orbits, nobody can say. Indeed, it is even now an open question as to whether gravity is due to push or pull. However that may be, we are quite certain from personal experience that what formerly was regarded as pure chance or "luck," and more of it bad than good, was but an expression of an universal law to which we are all subject by reason of our own natures. For we are all compounded of cosmic elements and answer to our greater environment at all points. But to the extent that we understand the laws at work about us we can use them to our own advantage, and through ourselves to the benefit of others. Thus we have conquered the hitherto unknown law of the tides, the law of optics, the laws of the air, and many of the finer forces of Nature such as electricity, radioactivity, etc., have come under our control by our knowledge of them. When, therefore, we understand the laws which control the seasons that are wet or dry, hot or cold, the forces which make for fertility or sterility of crops, we are at the root of the problem of the rise and fall in prices of commodities; and by other, but similar ways, we may even determine the fluctuations of stocks and shares on the market; and *mirabili dictu*, the winner of a race ! Let those who believe in "luck" stand on it to their undoing. The wise man will seek a surer footing.

CONCLUSION

I have said enough in the course of the foregoing pages to indicate that I do not propose to advance this "Silver Key" as one that will unlock the doors of all the halls of knowledge, or absolutely solve the problem of speculative investment. But I do claim that it is the only scientific attempt which has so far been made towards that end.

I claim, moreover, that it is capable of yielding far better net results than any system before the public, despite the fact that it entails a double selection and consequently loses one point on every winning investment made. It is, moreover, a system that does not give out. Something similar and doubtless superior to it has been privately circulated by me during the past ten years to students of astrology, and the information thus given I am not at liberty to publish. But in the interests of astrology, to which art, together with other Oriental studies, I have devoted the greater part of my life, it has been represented to me that some general statement of the main facts should be publicly communicated, and it is with the idea of creating an interest in the principle of astrology that this small work has been compiled.

TABLE OF SIDEREAL TIMES.

D M	January Sidereal Time H. M. S.	D M	February Sidereal Time H. M. S.	D M	March Sidereal Time H. M. S.	D M	April Sidereal Time H. M. S.
1	18 41 2	1	20 43 15	1	22 33 38	1	0 35 52
2	18 44 58	2	20 47 11	2	22 37 35	2	0 39 48
3	18 48 55	3	20 51 8	3	22 41 32	3	0 43 45
4	18 52 51	4	20 55 5	4	22 45 28	4	0 47 41
5	18 56 48	5	20 59 1	5	22 49 25	5	0 51 38
6	19 0 44	6	21 2 58	6	22 53 21	6	0 55 34
7	19 4 41	7	21 6 54	7	22 57 18	7	0 59 31
8	19 8 38	8	21 10 51	8	23 1 14	8	1 3 27
9	19 12 34	9	21 14 47	9	23 5 11	9	1 7 24
10	19 16 31	10	21 18 44	10	23 9 7	10	1 11 21
11	19 20 27	11	21 22 40	11	23 13 4	11	1 15 17
12	19 24 24	12	21 26 37	12	23 17 1	12	1 19 14
13	19 28 20	13	21 30 34	13	23 20 57	13	1 23 10
14	19 32 17	14	21 34 30	14	23 24 54	14	1 27 7
15	19 36 13	15	21 38 27	15	23 28 50	15	1 31 3
16	19 40 10	16	21 42 23	16	23 32 47	16	1 35 0
17	19 44 7	17	21 46 20	17	23 36 43	17	1 38 56
18	19 48 3	18	21 50 16	18	23 40 40	18	1 42 53
19	19 52 0	19	21 54 13	19	23 44 36	19	1 46 50
20	19 55 56	20	21 58 9	20	23 48 33	20	1 50 46
21	19 59 53	21	22 2 6	21	23 52 30	21	1 54 43
22	20 3 49	22	22 6 3	22	23 56 26	22	1 58 39
23	20 7 46	23	22 9 59	23	0 0 23	23	2 2 36
24	20 11 42	24	22 13 56	24	0 4 19	24	2 6 32
25	20 15 39	25	22 17 52	25	0 8 16	25	2 10 29
26	20 19 36	26	22 21 49	26	0 12 12	26	2 14 25
27	20 23 32	27	22 25 45	27	0 16 9	27	2 18 22
28	20 27 29	28	22 29 42	28	0 20 5	28	2 22 19
29	20 31 25			29	0 24 2	29	2 26 15
30	20 35 22			30	0 27 59	30	2 30 12
31	20 39 18			31	0 31 55		

If to the Sideral Time against each date you apply the following equations, the table may be made to serve for several years.

1911	Subtract	0 min. 57 secs.	1915	Subtract	0 min. 48 secs.
1912	,,	1 ,, 54 ,,	1916	,,	1 ,, 45 ,,
1913	Add	1 ,, 6 ,,	1917	Add	1 ,, 14 ,,
1914	,,	0 ,, 9 ,,	1918	,,	0 ,, 16 ,,

TABLE OF SIDEREAL TIMES.
(Continued).

\multicolumn{2}{c}{MAY}		\multicolumn{2}{c}{JUNE}		\multicolumn{2}{c}{JULY}		\multicolumn{2}{c}{AUGUST}	
D/M	Sidereal Time	D/M	Sidereal Time	D/M	Sidereal Time	D/M	Sidereal Time
	H. M. S.		H. M. S.		H. M. S.		H. M. S.
1	2 34 8	1	4 36 22	1	6 34 38	1	8 36 52
2	2 38 5	2	4 40 18	2	6 38 35	2	8 40 48
3	2 42 1	3	4 44 15	3	6 42 31	3	8 44 45
4	2 45 58	4	4 48 11	4	6 46 28	4	8 48 41
5	2 49 54	5	4 52 8	5	6 50 24	5	8 52 38
6	2 53 51	6	4 56 4	6	6 54 21	6	8 56 34
7	2 57 48	7	5 0 1	7	6 58 18	7	9 0 31
8	3 1 44	8	5 3 57	8	7 2 14	8	9 4 27
9	3 5 41	9	5 7 54	9	7 6 11	9	9 8 24
10	3 9 37	10	5 11 51	10	7 10 7	10	9 12 21
11	3 13 34	11	5 15 47	11	7 14 4	11	9 16 17
12	3 17 30	12	5 19 44	12	7 18 0	12	9 20 14
13	3 21 27	13	5 23 40	13	7 21 57	13	9 24 10
14	3 25 23	14	5 27 37	14	7 25 53	14	9 28 7
15	3 29 20	15	5 31 33	15	7 29 50	15	9 32 3
16	3 33 17	16	5 35 30	16	7 33 47	16	9 36 0
17	3 37 13	17	5 39 26	17	7 37 43	17	9 39 56
18	3 41 10	18	5 43 23	18	7 41 40	18	9 43 53
19	3 45 6	19	5 47 20	19	7 45 36	19	9 47 50
20	3 49 3	20	5 51 16	20	7 49 33	20	9 51 46
21	3 52 59	21	5 55 13	21	7 53 29	21	9 55 43
22	3 56 56	22	5 59 9	22	7 57 26	22	9 59 39
23	4 0 52	23	6 3 6	23	8 1 23	23	10 3 36
24	4 4 49	24	6 7 2	24	8 5 19	24	10 7 32
25	4 8 46	25	6 10 59	25	8 9 16	25	10 11 29
26	4 12 42	26	6 14 55	26	8 13 12	26	10 15 25
27	4 16 39	27	6 18 52	27	8 17 9	27	10 19 22
28	4 20 35	28	6 22 49	28	8 21 5	28	10 23 19
29	4 24 32	29	6 26 45	29	8 25 2	29	10 27 15
30	4 28 28	30	6 30 42	30	8 28 58	30	10 31 12
31	4 32 25			31	8 32 55	31	10 35 8

Table of Sidereal Times.
(Continued).

D M	September Sidereal Time	D M	October Sidereal Time	D M	November Sidereal Time	D M	December Sidereal Time
	H. M. S.		H. M. S.		H. M. S.		H. M. S.
1	10 39 5	1	12 37 21	1	14 39 35	1	16 37 51
2	10 43 1	2	12 41 18	2	14 43 31	2	16 41 48
3	10 46 58	3	12 45 14	3	14 47 28	3	16 45 44
4	10 50 54	4	12 49 11	4	14 51 24	4	16 49 41
5	10 54 51	5	12 53 8	5	14 55 21	5	16 53 37
6	10 58 48	6	12 57 4	6	14 59 17	6	16 57 34
7	11 2 44	7	13 1 1	7	15 3 14	7	17 1 31
8	11 6 41	8	13 4 57	8	15 7 10	8	17 5 27
9	11 10 37	9	13 8 54	9	15 11 7	9	17 9 24
10	11 14 34	10	13 12 50	10	15 15 4	10	17 13 20
11	11 18 30	11	13 16 47	11	15 19 0	11	17 17 17
12	11 22 27	12	13 20 43	12	15 22 57	12	17 21 13
13	11 26 23	13	13 24 40	13	15 26 53	13	17 25 10
14	11 30 20	14	13 28 37	14	15 30 50	14	17 29 6
15	11 34 16	15	13 32 33	15	15 34 46	15	17 33 13
16	11 38 13	16	13 36 30	16	15 38 43	16	17 37 0
17	11 42 10	17	13 40 26	17	15 42 39	17	17 40 56
18	11 46 6	18	13 44 23	18	15 46 36	18	17 44 53
19	11 50 3	19	13 48 19	19	15 50 33	19	17 48 49
20	11 53 59	20	13 52 16	20	15 54 29	20	17 52 46
21	11 57 56	21	13 56 12	21	15 58 26	21	17 56 42
22	12 1 52	22	14 0 9	22	16 2 22	22	18 0 39
23	12 5 49	23	14 4 6	23	16 6 19	23	18 4 36
24	12 9 45	24	14 8 2	24	16 10 15	24	18 8 32
25	12 13 42	25	14 11 59	25	16 14 12	25	18 12 29
26	12 17 38	26	14 15 55	26	16 18 8	26	18 16 25
27	12 21 35	27	14 19 52	27	16 22 5	27	18 20 22
28	12 25 32	28	14 23 48	28	16 26 2	28	18 24 18
29	12 29 28	29	14 27 45	29	16 29 58	29	18 28 15
30	12 33 25	30	14 31 41	30	16 33 55	30	18 32 11
		31	14 35 38			31	18 36 8

Table of Ascendants for Lat. 51° 32'

Serving for Kempton Park, Alexandra Park, Newbury, Epsom, Sandown Park, Hurst Park, Gatwick, Brighton, Lingfield, Bath, Salisbury, Windsor, Lewes, Ascot, Folkestone and the South of England.

Sidereal Time			Ascen. ♋		Sidereal Time			Ascen. ♌		Sidereal Time			Ascen. ♍	
H.	M.	S.	°	′	H.	M.	S.	°	′	H.	M.	S.	°	′
0	0	0	26	36	1	51	37	16	28	3	51	15	7	21
0	3	40	27	17	1	55	27	17	8	3	55	25	8	5
0	7	20	27	56	1	59	17	17	48	3	59	36	8	49
0	11	0	28	42	2	3	8	18	28	4	3	48	9	33
0	14	41	29	17	2	6	59	19	9	4	8	0	10	17
0	18	21	29	55	2	10	51	19	49	4	12	13	11	2
0	22	2	0 ♌ 34		2	14	44	20	29	4	16	26	11	46
0	25	42	1	14	2	18	37	21	10	4	20	40	12	30
0	29	23	1	55	2	22	31	21	51	4	24	55	13	15
0	33	4	2	33	2	26	25	22	32	4	29	10	14	0
0	36	45	3	15	2	30	20	23	14	4	33	26	14	45
0	40	26	3	54	2	34	16	23	55	4	37	42	15	30
0	44	8	4	33	2	38	13	24	36	4	41	59	16	15
0	47	50	5	12	2	42	10	25	17	4	46	16	17	0
0	51	32	5	52	2	46	8	25	58	4	50	34	17	45
0	55	14	6	30	2	50	7	26	40	4	54	52	18	30
0	58	57	7	9	2	54	7	27	22	4	59	10	19	16
1	2	40	7	50	2	58	7	28	4	5	3	29	20	3
1	6	23	8	30	3	2	8	28	46	5	7	49	20	49
1	10	7	9	9	3	6	9	29	28	5	12	9	21	35
1	13	51	9	48	3	10	12	0 ♍ 12		5	16	29	22	20
1	17	35	10	28	3	13	15	0	54	5	20	49	23	6
1	21	20	11	8	3	18	19	1	36	5	25	9	23	51
1	25	6	11	48	3	22	23	2	20	5	29	30	24	37
1	28	52	12	28	3	26	29	3	2	5	33	51	25	23
1	32	38	13	8	3	30	35	3	45	5	38	12	26	9
1	36	25	13	48	3	34	41	4	28	5	42	34	26	55
1	40	12	14	28	3	38	49	5	11	5	46	55	27	41
1	44	0	15	8	3	42	57	5	54	5	51	17	28	27
1	47	48	15	48	3	47	6	6	38	5	55	38	29	13
1	51	37	16	28	3	51	15	7	21	6	0	0	30	0

Table of Ascendants for Lat. 51° 32′
(Continued).

Sidereal Time			Ascen. ♎		Sidereal Time			Ascen. ♎		Sidereal Time			Ascen. ♏	
H.	M.	S.	°	′	H.	M.	S.	°	′	H.	M.	S.	°	′
6	0	0	0	0	8	8	45	22	40	10	8	23	13	33
6	4	22	0	47	8	12	54	23	24	10	12	12	14	13
6	8	43	1	33	8	17	3	24	7	10	16	0	14	53
6	13	5	2	19	8	21	11	24	50	10	19	48	15	33
6	17	26	3	5	8	25	19	25	34	10	23	35	16	13
6	21	48	3	51	8	29	26	26	18	10	27	22	16	52
6	26	9	4	37	8	33	31	27	1	10	31	8	17	32
6	30	30	5	23	8	37	37	27	44	10	34	54	18	13
6	34	51	6	9	8	41	41	28	26	10	38	40	18	52
6	39	11	6	55	8	45	45	29	8	10	42	25	19	31
6	43	31	7	40	8	49	48	29	50	10	46	9	20	11
6	47	51	8	26	8	53	51	0 ♏	32	10	49	53	20	50
6	52	11	9	12	8	57	52	1	15	10	53	37	21	30
6	56	31	9	58	9	1	53	1	58	10	57	20	22	9
7	0	50	10	43	9	5	53	2	39	11	1	3	22	49
7	5	8	11	28	9	9	53	3	21	11	4	46	23	28
7	9	26	12	14	9	13	52	4	3	11	8	28	24	8
7	13	44	12	59	9	17	50	4	44	11	12	10	24	47
7	18	1	13	45	9	21	47	5	26	11	15	52	25	17
7	22	18	14	30	9	25	44	6	7	11	19	34	26	6
7	26	34	15	15	9	29	40	6	48	11	23	15	26	45
7	30	50	16	0	9	33	35	7	29	11	26	56	27	25
7	35	5	16	45	9	37	29	8	9	11	30	37	28	5
7	39	20	17	30	9	41	23	8	50	11	34	18	28	44
7	43	34	18	15	9	45	16	9	31	11	37	58	29	24
7	47	47	18	59	9	49	9	10	11	11	41	39	0 ♐	3
7	52	0	19	43	9	53	1	10	51	11	45	19	0	43
7	56	12	20	27	9	56	52	11	32	11	49	0	1	23
8	0	24	21	11	10	0	43	12	12	11	52	40	2	3
8	4	35	21	56	10	4	33	12	53	11	56	20	2	43
8	8	45	22	40	10	8	23	13	33	12	0	0	3	23

Table of Ascendants for Lat. 51° 32'
(Continued).

Sidereal Time			Ascen. ♐		Sidereal Time			Ascen. ♐		Sidereal Time			Ascen. ♑	
H.	M.	S.	°	'	H.	M.	S.	°	'	H.	M.	S.	°	'
12	0	0	3	23	13	51	37	25	20	15	51	15	27	15
12	3	40	4	4	13	55	27	26	10	15	55	25	28	42
12	7	20	4	45	13	59	17	27	2	15	59	36	0 ♒ 11	
12	11	0	5	26	14	3	8	27	53	16	3	48	1	42
12	14	41	6	7	14	6	59	28	45	16	8	0	3	16
12	18	21	6	48	14	10	51	29	36	16	12	13	4	53
12	22	2	7	29	14	14	44	0 ♑ 29		16	16	26	6	32
12	25	42	8	10	14	18	37	1	23	16	20	40	8	13
12	29	23	8	51	14	22	31	2	18	16	24	55	9	57
12	33	4	9	33	14	26	25	3	14	16	29	10	11	44
12	36	45	10	15	14	30	20	4	11	16	33	26	13	34
12	40	26	10	57	14	34	16	5	9	16	37	42	15	26
12	44	8	11	40	14	38	13	6	7	16	41	59	17	20
12	47	50	12	22	14	42	10	7	6	16	46	16	19	18
12	51	32	13	4	14	46	8	8	6	16	50	34	21	22
12	55	14	13	47	14	50	7	9	8	16	54	52	23	29
12	58	57	14	30	14	54	7	10	11	16	59	10	25	36
13	2	40	15	14	14	58	7	11	15	17	3	29	27	46
13	6	23	15	59	15	2	8	12	20	17	7	49	0 ♓ 0	
13	10	7	16	44	15	6	9	13	27	17	12	9	2	19
13	13	51	17	29	15	10	12	14	35	17	16	29	4	40
13	17	35	18	14	15	14	15	15	43	17	20	49	7	2
13	21	20	19	0	15	18	19	16	52	17	25	9	9	26
13	25	6	19	45	15	22	23	18	3	17	29	30	11	54
13	28	52	20	31	15	26	29	19	16	17	33	51	14	24
13	32	38	21	18	15	30	35	20	32	17	38	12	17	0
13	36	25	22	6	15	34	41	21	48	17	42	34	19	33
13	40	12	22	54	15	38	49	23	8	17	46	55	22	6
13	44	0	23	42	15	42	57	24	29	17	51	17	24	40
13	47	48	24	31	15	47	6	25	51	17	55	38	27	20
13	51	37	25	20	15	51	15	27	15	18	0	0	30	0

TABLE OF ASCENDANTS FOR LAT. 51° 32'
(Continued).

Sidereal Time			Ascen. ♈		Sidereal Time			Ascen. ♊		Sidereal Time			Ascen. ♋	
H.	M.	S.	°	′	H.	M.	S.	°	′	H.	M.	S.	°	′
18	0	0	0	0	20	8	45	2	45	22	8	23	4	38
18	4	22	2	39	20	12	54	4	9	22	12	12	5	28
18	8	43	5	19	20	17	3	5	32	22	16	0	6	17
18	13	5	7	55	20	21	11	6	53	22	19	48	7	5
18	17	26	10	29	20	25	19	8	12	22	23	35	7	53
18	21	48	13	2	20	29	26	9	27	22	27	22	8	42
18	26	9	15	56	20	33	31	10	43	22	31	8	9	29
18	30	30	18	6	20	37	37	11	58	22	34	54	10	16
18	34	51	20	34	20	41	41	13	9	22	38	40	11	2
18	39	11	22	59	20	45	45	14	18	22	42	25	11	47
18	43	31	25	22	20	49	48	15	25	22	46	9	12	31
18	47	51	27	42	20	53	51	16	32	22	49	53	13	16
18	52	11	29	58	20	57	52	17	39	22	53	37	14	1
18	56	31	2 ♉	13	21	1	53	18	44	22	57	20	14	45
19	0	50	4	24	21	5	53	19	48	23	1	3	15	28
19	5	8	6	30	21	9	53	20	51	23	4	46	16	11
19	9	26	8	36	21	13	52	21	53	23	8	28	16	54
19	13	44	10	40	21	17	50	22	53	23	12	10	17	37
19	18	1	12	39	21	21	47	23	52	23	15	52	18	20
19	22	18	14	35	21	25	44	24	51	23	19	34	19	3
19	26	34	16	28	21	29	40	25	48	23	23	15	19	45
19	30	50	18	17	21	33	35	26	44	23	26	56	20	26
19	35	5	20	3	21	37	29	27	40	23	30	37	21	8
19	39	20	21	48	21	41	23	28	34	23	34	18	21	50
19	43	34	23	29	21	45	16	29	29	23	37	58	22	31
19	47	47	25	9	21	49	9	0 ♋	22	23	41	39	23	12
19	52	0	26	45	21	53	1	1	15	23	45	19	23	53
19	56	12	28	18	21	56	52	2	7	23	49	0	24	32
20	0	24	29	49	22	0	43	2	57	23	52	40	25	15
20	4	35	1 ♊	19	22	4	33	3	48	23	56	20	25	56
20	8	45	2	45	22	8	23	4	38	24	0	0	26	36

Table of Ascendants for Lat. 53° 25'
(Continued).

Serving for Liverpool, Manchester, York, Hull, Nottingham, Derby, Haydock Park, Ripon, Lincoln, etc.

Sidereal Time			Ascen. ♋		Sidereal Time			Ascen. ♌		Sidereal Time			Ascen. ♍	
H.	M.	S.	°	'	H.	M.	S.	°	'	H.	M.	S.	°	'
0	0	0	28	13	1	51	37	17	32	3	51	15	7	54
0	3	40	28	46	1	55	27	18	11	3	55	25	8	37
0	7	20	29	25	1	59	17	18	51	3	59	36	9	20
0	11	0	0 ♌	14	2	3	8	19	30	4	3	48	10	3
0	14	41	0	49	2	6	59	20	9	4	8	0	10	47
0	18	21	1	25	2	10	51	20	48	4	12	13	11	30
0	22	2	2	7	2	14	44	21	37	4	16	26	12	13
0	25	42	2	42	2	18	37	22	8	4	20	40	12	56
0	29	23	3	26	2	22	31	22	47	4	24	55	13	40
0	33	4	4	4	2	26	25	23	28	4	29	10	14	24
0	36	45	4	41	2	30	20	24	8	4	33	26	15	8
0	40	26	5	19	2	34	16	24	48	4	37	42	15	52
0	44	8	5	58	2	38	13	25	28	4	41	59	16	36
0	47	50	6	36	2	42	10	26	8	4	46	16	17	19
0	51	32	7	14	2	46	8	26	48	4	50	34	18	4
0	55	14	7	53	2	50	7	27	29	4	54	52	18	49
0	58	57	8	32	2	54	7	28	10	4	59	10	19	33
1	2	40	9	10	2	58	7	28	51	5	3	29	20	17
1	6	23	9	47	3	2	8	29	32	5	7	49	21	1
1	10	7	10	25	3	6	9	0 ♍	13	5	12	9	21	46
1	13	51	11	5	3	10	12	0	54	5	16	29	22	31
1	17	35	11	43	3	14	15	1	36	5	20	49	23	16
1	21	20	12	22	3	18	19	2	17	5	25	9	24	0
1	25	6	13	0	3	22	23	2	59	5	29	30	24	45
1	28	52	13	39	3	26	29	3	41	5	33	51	25	30
1	32	38	14	18	3	30	35	4	23	5	38	12	26	15
1	36	25	14	56	3	34	41	5	5	5	42	34	27	0
1	40	12	15	35	3	38	49	5	47	5	46	55	27	45
1	44	0	16	14	3	42	57	6	30	5	51	17	28	30
1	47	48	16	53	3	47	6	7	12	5	55	38	29	15
1	51	37	17	32	3	51	15	7	54	6	0	0	30	0

Table of Ascendants for Lat. 53° 25'
(Continued).

Sidereal Time			Ascen. ♎		Sidereal Time			Ascen. ♎		Sidereal Time			Ascen. ♏	
H.	M.	S.	°	′	H.	M.	S.	°	′	H.	M.	S.	°	′
6	0	0	0	0	8	8	45	22	6	10	8	23	12	28
6	4	22	0	45	8	12	54	22	48	10	12	12	13	6
6	8	43	1	30	8	17	3	23	30	10	16	0	13	45
6	13	5	2	15	8	21	11	24	13	10	19	48	14	25
6	17	26	3	0	8	25	19	24	55	10	23	35	15	4
6	21	48	3	45	8	29	26	25	37	10	27	22	15	42
6	26	9	4	30	8	33	31	26	19	10	31	8	16	21
6	30	30	5	15	8	37	37	27	1	10	34	54	17	0
6	34	51	6	0	8	41	41	27	43	10	38	40	17	39
6	39	11	6	44	8	45	45	28	24	10	42	25	18	17
6	43	31	7	29	8	49	48	29	6	10	46	9	18	55
6	47	51	8	14	8	53	51	29	47	10	49	53	19	34
6	52	11	8	59	8	57	52	0♏28		10	53	37	20	13
6	56	31	9	43	9	1	53	1	9	10	57	20	20	51
7	0	50	10	27	9	5	53	1	50	11	1	3	21	30
7	5	8	11	11	9	9	53	2	31	11	4	46	22	8
7	9	26	11	56	9	13	52	3	12	11	8	28	22	46
7	13	44	12	40	9	17	50	3	52	11	12	10	23	24
7	18	1	13	24	9	21	47	4	32	11	15	22	24	2
7	22	18	14	8	9	25	44	5	12	11	19	34	24	40
7	26	34	14	52	9	29	40	5	52	11	23	15	25	19
7	30	50	15	36	9	33	35	6	32	11	26	56	25	59
7	35	5	16	20	9	37	29	7	13	11	30	37	26	38
7	39	20	17	4	9	41	23	7	53	11	34	18	27	15
7	43	34	17	47	9	45	16	8	33	11	37	58	27	53
7	47	47	18	30	9	49	9	9	12	11	41	39	28	32
7	52	0	19	13	9	53	1	9	51	11	45	19	29	11
7	56	12	19	57	9	56	52	10	30	11	49	0	29	53
8	0	24	20	40	10	0	43	11	9	11	52	40	0♐	35
8	4	35	21	23	10	4	33	11	48	11	56	20	1	11
8	8	45	22	6	10	8	23	12	28	12	0	0	1	48

Table of Ascendants for Lat. 53° 25'
(Continued).

Sidereal Time			Ascen. ♐		Sidereal Time			Ascen. ♑		Sidereal Time			Ascen. ♒	
H.	M.	S.	°	'	H.	M.	S.	°	'	H.	M.	S.	°	'
12	0	0	1	48	13	51	37	23	6	15	51	15	24	15
12	3	40	2	27	13	55	27	23	55	15	55	25	25	41
12	7	20	3	6	13	59	17	24	43	15	59	36	27	10
12	11	0	3	46	14	3	8	25	33	16	3	48	28	41
12	14	41	4	25	14	6	59	26	23	16	8	0	0 ♒ 14	
12	18	21	5	6	14	10	51	27	14	16	12	13	1	50
12	22	2	5	46	14	14	44	28	6	16	16	26	3	30
12	25	42	6	26	14	18	37	28	59	16	20	40	5	13
12	29	23	7	6	14	22	31	29	52	16	24	55	6	58
12	33	4	7	46	14	26	25	0 ♑ 46		16	29	10	8	46
12	36	45	8	27	14	30	20	1	41	16	33	26	10	38
12	40	26	9	8	14	34	16	2	36	16	37	42	12	32
12	44	8	9	49	14	38	13	3	33	16	41	59	14	31
12	47	50	10	30	14	42	10	4	30	16	46	16	16	33
12	51	32	11	12	14	46	8	5	29	16	50	34	18	40
12	55	14	11	54	14	50	7	6	29	16	54	52	20	50
12	58	57	12	36	14	54	7	7	30	16	59	10	23	4
13	2	40	13	19	14	58	7	8	32	17	3	29	25	21
13	6	23	14	2	15	2	8	9	35	17	7	49	27	42
13	10	7	14	45	15	6	9	10	39	17	12	9	0 ♓ 8	
13	13	51	15	28	15	10	12	11	45	17	16	29	2	37
13	17	35	16	12	15	14	15	12	52	17	20	49	5	10
13	21	20	16	55	15	18	19	14	1	17	25	9	7	46
13	25	6	17	41	15	22	23	15	11	17	29	30	10	24
13	28	52	18	26	15	26	29	16	23	17	33	51	13	7
13	32	38	19	11	15	30	35	17	37	17	38	12	15	52
13	36	25	19	57	15	34	41	18	53	17	42	34	18	38
13	40	12	20	44	15	38	49	20	10	17	46	55	21	27
13	44	0	21	31	15	42	57	21	29	17	51	17	24	17
13	47	48	22	18	15	47	6	22	51	17	55	38	27	8
13	51	37	23	6	15	51	15	24	15	18	0	0	30	0

TABLE OF ASCENDANTS FOR LAT. 53° 25'
(Continued).

Sidereal Time			Ascen. ♈		Sidereal Time			Ascen. ♊		Sidereal Time			Ascen. ♋	
H.	M.	S.	°	′	H.	M.	S.	°	′	H.	M.	S.	°	′
18	0	0	0	0	20	8	45	5	45	22	8	23	6	54
18	4	22	2	52	20	12	54	7	9	22	12	12	7	42
18	8	43	5	43	20	17	3	8	31	22	16	0	8	29
18	13	5	8	33	20	21	11	9	50	22	19	48	9	16
18	17	26	11	22	20	25	19	11	7	22	23	35	10	3
18	21	48	14	8	20	29	26	12	23	22	27	22	10	49
18	26	9	16	53	20	33	31	13	37	22	31	8	11	34
18	30	30	19	36	20	37	37	14	49	22	34	54	12	19
18	34	51	22	14	20	41	41	15	59	22	38	40	13	5
18	39	11	24	50	20	45	45	17	8	22	42	25	13	48
18	43	31	27	23	20	49	48	18	15	22	46	9	14	32
18	47	51	29	52	20	53	51	19	21	22	49	53	15	15
18	52	11	2 ♉ 18		20	57	52	20	25	22	53	37	15	58
18	56	31	4	39	21	1	53	21	28	22	57	20	16	41
19	0	50	6	56	21	5	53	22	30	23	1	3	17	24
19	5	8	9	10	21	9	53	23	31	23	4	46	18	6
19	9	26	11	20	21	13	52	24	31	23	8	28	18	48
19	13	44	13	27	21	17	50	25	30	23	12	10	19	30
19	18	1	15	29	21	21	47	26	27	23	15	52	20	11
19	22	18	17	28	21	25	44	27	24	23	19	34	20	52
19	26	34	19	22	21	29	40	28	19	23	23	15	21	33
19	30	50	21	14	21	33	35	29	14	23	26	56	22	14
19	35	5	23	2	21	37	29	0 ♋ 8		23	30	37	22	54
19	39	20	24	47	21	41	23	1	1	23	34	18	23	34
19	43	34	26	30	21	45	16	1	54	23	37	58	24	14
19	47	47	28	10	21	49	9	2	46	23	41	39	24	54
19	52	0	29	46	21	53	1	3	37	23	45	19	25	35
19	56	12	1 ♊ 19		21	56	52	4	27	23	49	0	26	14
20	0	24	2	50	22	0	43	5	17	23	52	40	26	54
20	4	35	4	19	22	4	33	6	5	23	56	20	27	33
20	8	45	5	45	22	8	23	6	54	24	0	0	28	12

A 50% reduction of the first page of the Arcana.
See the Publisher's Note on pg. 126.

THE ARCANA or STOCK AND SHARE KEY BY   SEPHARIAL

The RADIX of any company is the noon of the date and place of registration of that Company, whereby, under the laws of the country the promotors are given powers to form the company and proceed with business.

The RADIX of a Stock Exchange IS THE NOON OF THE DATE OF FOUNDING. The charts for New York and London are attached hereto and will serve as examples of all others, FROM THIS RADIX or root figure of the heavens a variety of influences are by natural process of celestial motions indicated. These are found to depend altogether upon the Sun, which is the controlling center of their interactions. The Sun's MAN MOTION IS 59 minutes and eight seconds per day. The measure of TIME IS ONE DAY FOR A YEAR. Thus the influences arising out of the movement of the bodies in relation to the Sun will influence successive years of the Company, the indications arising in the second day affecting the second year, those formed on the third day influence the third year, and so on continuously.

SOLAR MOTION: THE APPARENT MOTION OF THE SUN AS SEEN FROM THE EARTH is slightly variable, according to the season of the year. This is due to the fact that the apparent orbit of the Sun is not concentric with the

The Arcana
or
Stock and Share Key

by
Sepharial

Publisher's note

Sepharial's various Arcana were sold by subscription, with the requirement they be kept private. My source for this Arcana was John Ballantrae's Universe Bookstore. I do not know from where he obtained it.

The copy he sold me was typescript, many generations copied. There are several things of interest about it: It appears to have been made on an electric typewriter, and the ribbon used was nylon, or possibly silk. I once had use of such a machine, many years ago. It was clear to me that it was NOT made on a manual typewriter, and the ribbon used was NOT made of cotton. On page 127 you will find the word, "center", which is an American spelling.

The majority of the present Arcana seems to date from 1913-14. The final three pages of the Ballantrae original, starting with "The Chart of the Heavens for London" appear to be from a later date.

In Ballantrae's copy, the two charts were hand-drawn. They appear to have originally been on separate pages, but I found them on a single sheet. On both charts, Pluto has been added. A modified Mars symbol was used to denote it. In addition, the word, "PLUTO" was added to both. The handwriting does not appear to match that of the charts shown in Sepharial's other books.

Such are some of the problems with texts of this sort.

I have reset the text, but have followed the original formatting as closely as possible.

David R. Roell

The Arcana
or
Stock and Share Key

The RADIX of any company is the noon of the date and place of registration of that Company, whereby, under the laws of the country the promoters are given powers to form the company and proceed with business.

The RADIX of a Stock Exchange IS THE NOON OF THE DATE OF FOUNDING. The charts for New York and London are attached hereto and will serve as examples of all others. FROM THIS RADIX or root figure of the heavens a variety of influences are by natural process of celestial motions indicated. These are found to depend altogether upon the Sun, which is the controlling center of their interactions. The Sun's MEAN MOTION IS 59 minutes and eight seconds per day. The measure of TIME IS ONE DAY FOR A YEAR. Thus the influences arising out of the movement of the bodies in relation to the Sun will influence successive years of the Company, the indications arising in the second day affecting the second year, those formed on the third day influence the third year, and so on continuously.

SOLAR MOTION: THE APPARENT MOTION OF THE SUN AS SEEN FROM THE EARTH is slightly variable, according to the season of the year. This is due to the fact that the apparent orbit of the Sun is not concentric with the earth but is slightly removed therefrom, thus producing an eccentricity of its apparent motion about the earth, and this may amount to as much as one degree and fifty six minutes either way, as compared with its mean, or average motion, which is 59 minutes 8 seconds per day. It has been found in a great number of tests that the MEAN MOTION OF THE

The Arcana, or Stock and Share Key

SUN IS THE CORRECT MEASURE TO BE OBSERVED, AND THE SUN REQUIRES 365¼ days to complete the circle of 360 degrees we have a mean motion of 59 minutes 8 seconds per day.

This amount is multiplied by the number of years from the radix or date of registration and added to the Sun's place in the radix (called Sun r), also the Midheaven, and to the Moon r. The other planets are in the same way carried forward through the zodiac at the same rate as the Sun and maintain their radical relations with the Sun thereby, but in the course of their progress from day to day at this uniform rate, they form aspects to the radical places of the Sun, Midheaven, Moon, and ascendant of the radix. These aspects are called DIRECTIONAL ASPECTS and they INFLUENCE THE AFFAIRS OF THE COMPANY OR BUSINESS OF ANY EXCHANGE ACCORDING TO THEIR SEVERAL NATURES.

THE PRIME SIGNIFICATOR OF ANY CHART IS THAT PLANET WHICH RULES THE SIGN IN WHICH THE SUN IS FOUND. Thus, in the chart for the New York Stock Exchange, the Sun is in the sign Taurus. This sign is rules by Venus, and Venus therefore becomes PRIME SIGNIFICATOR.

THE SECONDARY SIGNIFICATOR IS THE PLANET WHICH RULES THE DECANATE IN WHICH THE PRIME SIGNIFICATOR HAPPENS TO BE PASSING THROUGH IN THE COURSE OF ITS DAILY MOTION IN THE HEAVENS as shown in the ephemeris for the current year. The use of these significators will be given further on in this exposition. FIRST, let us look at the method of DIRECTING which has been found to be a guide TO THE GENERAL MARKET OUTLOOK.

The New York chart is set for noon on the 17th of May, 1792 as shown in the map herewith. Now at the tragic assassination of President Abraham Lincoln we find the years from the above date of founding to the date of that event, APRIL 14TH, 1865, to be a period of 73 YEARS ONE MONTH. This at the rate of 59' 8" per day (year) is 72 degrees 2 minutes and being added to the radical Midheaven of Taurus 28 we come to the 11th degree of the sign LEO, AND THE ASCENDANT UNDER THIS M.C. is the 5th degree of SCORPIO. The ascen-

The Arcana, or Stock and Share Key

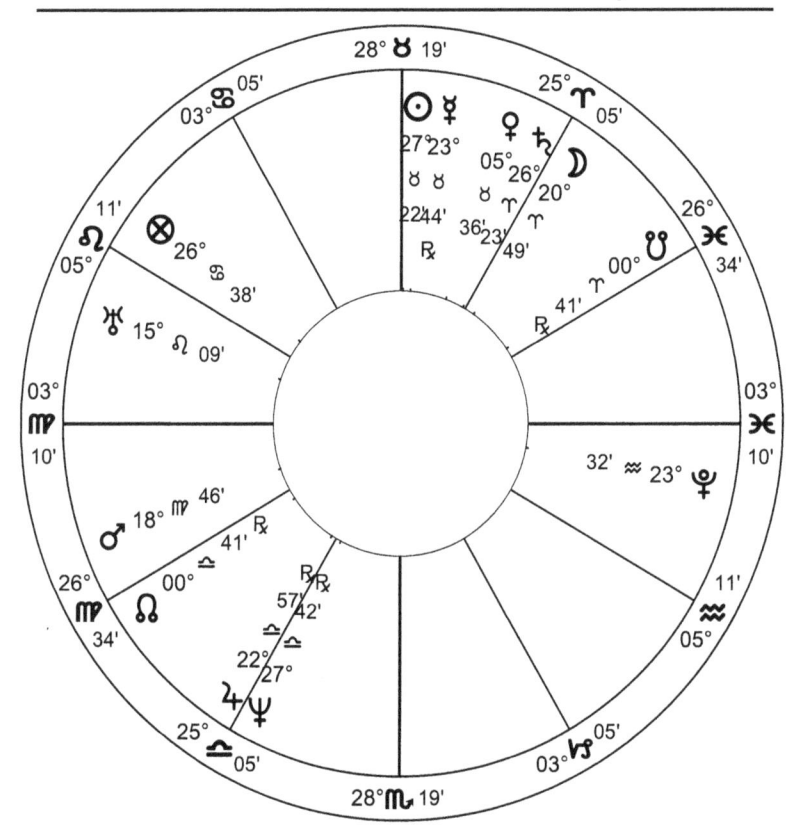

New York Stock Exchange, May 17, 1792, noon LMT, Wall Street.
Placidus Houses, Mean Node.

dant was therefore in opposition to Venus radical. Referring to the ephemeris for 1865 we find that on the very day Neptune, the author of plots and schemes, was in Aries 8:40 and therefore exactly on the place of the Moon radical.*

AXIOM ONE

Planets in transit over the radical places of the SUN, MOON, MIDHEAVEN, AND ASCENDANT OF THE CHART have influence on the course of events according to their natures, and so effect the VALUE OF SECURITIES. In November 1857 there was a considerable panic (financial panic) on the Exchange. Time 65 years 6 months. M.C. progress to Leo 2:34, Asc. in Libra 27. The Asc. is opposed to SAT-

---
*This appears to be a mistake on Sepharial's part. The lunar position he cites was true of the 16th - *Publisher*

URN and in conjunction with NEPTUNE. Venus was then in the end of LIBRA (CONJ. NEPTUNE r) and SATURN was in CANCER in square aspect to Venus Midmonth in November 1857. URANUS was in transit over M.C. radical.

AXIOM TWO

DIRECTIONS OF THE GENERAL SIGNIFICATORS, SUN, MOON, M.C. AND ASC., TO AFFLICTING ASPECTS (SQUARE OR OPPOSITION) OF MALEFIC PLANETS WILL CAUSE GREAT DEPRESSION OF SECURITIES.

AXIOM THREE

The ephemeris aspects to the PRIME SIGNIFICATOR WILL DEFINE THE PROBABLE TIME FOR THIS DEPRESSION. The Railway Strike of August 1890 at 98 years 3 months from the foundation of the chart shows M.C. in Virgo 5. Saturn was then in transit through that degree of the zodiac.

AXIOM FOUR

Saturn IN CONJUNCTION, OR SQUARE OR OPPOSITION-by transit-to ANY OF THE RADICAL PLACES OF THE GENERAL SIGNIFICATORS, OR TO THEIR PROGRESSED PLACES, WILL CAUSE A SERIOUS DEPRESSION. In August 1914 Saturn was in Gemini 28 in square to Mars in Virgo 28. The M.C. of the chart had progressed to Virgo 28. Mars was therefore in transit over the Progressed M.C. and Saturn was in square to it. Mars is here the cause of the excitement and Saturn that of the depression.

EFFECTS OF PLANETS. NEPTUNE in BAD ASPECT CAUSES BEARISH SALES AND HIS ACTION IS GENERALLY DUE TO "RINGS" AND PROFESSIONAL COMBINES MOVING FOR A LOWER BUYING LEVEL. ITS GOOD ASPECTS ADVANCE VALUES FROM THE SAME CAUSES.

URANUS USUALLY BRINGS IN THE GOVERNMENT BROKER AND SHOWS OFFICIAL MANIPULATION OF THE MARKET. In good aspect it makes for buying, and in bad aspect for selling. At such times keep one eye on Uranus and the other on the Government Broker.

SATURN steadies the market when in good aspect, but greatly depresses it when in evil aspect to the SIGNIFICATORS, RADICAL AND PROGRESSED.

The Arcana, or Stock and Share Key

JUPITER enhances values by its conjunction or good aspects, and causes heavy selling for profits when in bad aspect. It deflates what it previously had inflated.

MARS stimulates the market and in good aspect causes sharp rises and a brisk market, while in evil aspect it causes sharp depressions. Neither are enduring.

VENUS in good aspect gives equable values and a steady rise in values but is not enduring. In bad aspect it causes a flat and lifeless market.

MERCURY causes rises when in good aspect by 'reports' and market talk and makes for brisk but small improvements. In bad aspect it causes quick in and out buying and selling with balance against values.

AXIOM

All planets in good aspect enhance values according to their several natures, the major planets being more powerful than the minor. Jupiter, Mars and Venus, have the greatest power for good when in good aspect, but Venus has not the same power in transit as in Direction.

THE DECANATES

Sign						
Aries	0 to 10	Mars	11 to 20	Sun	21 to 30	Venus
Taurus	0 to 10	Mercury	11 to 20	Moon	21 to 30	Saturn
Gemini	0 to 10	Jupiter	11 to 20	Mars	21 to 30	Sun
Cancer	0 to 10	Venus	11 to 20	Mercury	21 to 30	Moon
Leo	0 to 10	Saturn	11 to 20	Jupiter	21 to 30	Mercury
Virgo	0 to 10	Sun	11 to 20	Venus	21 to 30	Mercury
Libra	0 to 10	Moon	11 to 20	Saturn	21 to 30	Jupiter
Scorpio	0 to 10	Mars	11 to 20	Sun	21 to 30	Venus
Sagittarius	0 to 10	Mercury	11 to 20	Moon	21 to 30	Saturn
Capricorn	0 to 10	Jupiter	11 to 20	Mars	21 to 30	Sun
Aquarius	0 to 10	Venus	11 to 20	Mercury	21 to 30	Moon
Pisces	0 to 10	Saturn	11 to 20	Jupiter	21 to 30	Mars

These decans are parts of the signs each ten degrees in extent and their rulers are set against them. When the PRIME SIGNIFICATOR is passing through any decan it is the guest of the ruler of that decan and is subject in some measure to the aspects affecting that ruler so long as the PRIME SIGNIFICATOR remains in that Decan. These can be found in the ephemeris from week to week throughout the year and FORM THE BASIS OF "FLUCTUATIONS", while being subject to the general tone of the market indicated by the DIRECTIONS of the general significators and the major transits over them. For example:

> At the time of the railway strike in 1890, we find Saturn in transit over the M.C. Progressed in Virgo 5 and in square aspect to Mars, then in Sagittarius 5, and near to the square of Neptune in Gemini 6, while Uranus was in transit over Jupiter's place in the radix on the cusp of the third house (Railways). But Venus, the PRIME SIGNIFICATOR, was then in the end of Virgo and not in aspect to any planet in the heavens. The Secondary Significator is Mercury, which rules the last decan of Virgo, where Venus is guest. Now we find Mercury was then in conjunction with Saturn in Virgo 5 and therefore square to Mars and square to Neptune in the heavens at the time. Here are adequate causes for predicting a severe set-back.

NATURE OF ASPECTS

The good aspects are the trine of 120 degrees, the sextile of 60 degrees, the conjunction of Jupiter and Venus and the PARALLELS of these also. The bad aspects are the opposition of 180 degrees, the square of 90, the sesquiquadrate of 135, and the semi-square of 45. Also the conjunctions of SATURN AND ITS PARALLELS. The planets URANUS, NEPTUNE, AND MARS, ACT VARIOUSLY WHEN IN CONJUNCTION AND ARE LARGELY UNDER THE DIRECTION OF PRIMARY INDICATIONS CURRENT AT THE TIME.

AXIOM

ALL PLANETS IN GOOD ASPECT ACT TO ENHANCE VALUES. ALL PLANETS IN BAD ASPECT ACT TO DEPRECIATE VALUES. BUT JUPITER IS THE GREATEST EXPANDER, AND SATURN THE GREATEST DEPRESSOR OF THE MARKETS.

AXIOM

A PLANET IS JUDGED BY ITS OWN NATURE, AND AN ASPECT BY ITS OWN NATURE.

A BOOM on the market is produced from a succession of good aspects to the PRIME SIGNIFICATOR OR ITS DECAN RULER. WHEN BOTH ARE WELL ASPECTED THE EXTENT IS DOUBLED. It is usually terminated by a change of decan, if not sooner by a break of benefic causes.

The Arcana, or Stock and Share Key

A SLUMP is caused by a succession of bad aspects to the Significator and its Decan Ruler.

TRANSITION POINTS are formed midway between a good and a bad aspect to the same indicator. Thus:

Venus on the 8th of the month is opposition Jupiter.
On the 11th is sextile Saturn.
On the 20th it is semi-square Mercury.
On the 30th it is semi-square Neptune.

Therefore we should expect a fair amount of selling or realizing of profits. This would be followed, about the 9th or 10th, by a steadying influence under the approaching sextile of Saturn and Saturn would give a steady upward trend until the 15th-16th, which is the transition point between Saturn and the next aspecting planet Mercury. At this time the market turns and begins to be talked down, and under Venus semi-square Neptune it continues down to the 28th. Here it forms another transition point and proceeds to the sextile of Mercury, which it reaches on August 2nd. These aspects are formed in July 1914. After the 2nd of August the planet Venus meets the conjunction with Mars in Virgo on the 5th, and then goes to the square of Saturn, the change of Decan taking place on August 2nd and changing the good influence of Mercury to that of Mars (war). Venus, being then in the last decan of Virgo, ruled by Mercury, we have further indication of Mercury conjunction Neptune at that time, showing a state of chaos. The direction for 122 years 3 months is 120 degrees 29 minutes and it will be seen that if we add this amount to the M.C. of the radix (Taurus 28) we arrive at just this same position in the zodiac, namely Virgo 28, which is occupied by Mars and Venus in square aspect to Saturn in Gemini at that time. So we have good reason for anticipating a considerable stir in the markets of the world and a great depreciation of values.

DAILY FLUCTUATIONS CAN ONLY BE FOLLOWED WITH SUCCESS by those who are on the spot and watching the clock and ticker. For it will be found that the course of the market follows the MERIDIAN TRANSIT of the planets and the aspects formed to them by the others at the time of their transit. Taking the Sun as indicating noon position, it will be seen that some planets precede the Sun and others follow it. Thus at the beginning of August 1914 we have Sun opposition Uranus, on the second of the month, followed by the Sun semi-square Saturn on the 6th. The heaviest point should therefore be on the 4th, or mid-distance between the aspects. On that date Mercury passed over the MERIDIAN 19 degrees, or 1 hour 16 minutes before noon, in opposition at the time to the Moon. About 24 minutes later Neptune passed the MERIDIAN. Then came the Sun at Noon in Opposition to Uranus and approaching the semi-square of Saturn. Here we have the big depression. It is followed by the transit of Jupiter over the lower Meridian at 12:28 or 28 minutes after noon. Then there is a lot of selling done. Then comes Mars and Venus, in close conjunction in Virgo 23-24 degrees in sextile to Mercury in Cancer 22, but also coming to the square of Saturn in Gemini. This would be about 3:50 P.M. Local Time, and it then became a pressing question as to Peace or War - Mars or Venus - a question that would serve no market any good.

THE CHART OF ANY PRIVATE COMPANY OR SYNDICATE is to be judged by exactly the same set of indications, and the share values of such company, if offered on the open market, will follow the specific indications belonging to and derived from that chart, subject only to the general indications of the Exchange Chart and the ephemeral transits as already set forth. But each set of indications must be taken account of in THIS ORDER:

1. PRIMARY INDICATIONS, derived from directions of the Midheaven, etc. for the current year.

2. TRANSITS OVER THESE PRIMARY POINTS - Sun, Moon, Midheaven, Asc., both radical and progressed, the latter being the more important in relation to the current period.

3. ASPECTS FORMED TO THE PRIME SIGNIFICATOR in the ephemeris from day to day or from week to week, as the case may be.

4. ASPECTS FORMED TO THE RULER OF THE DECAN THEN HELD BY THE PRIME SIGNIFICATOR.

All of these, which being duly noted, will form a concat-

The Arcana, or Stock and Share Key

enation or depending series of influences which will inevitably lead to correct estimation of the TREND OF THE MARKET.

5. Having decided to buy or sell, enter the market WHEN THE MERIDIAN TRANSITS ARE AGREEABLE TO THE CURRENT INDICATIONS FROM WHICH YOUR DECISION WAS MADE. This is the whole business of stock and share trading by chart.

SIGN RULERS

The Sun being in Capricorn or Aquarius - Saturn is Prime Significator.

The Sun being in Sagit or Pisces - Jupiter is Prime Significator.

The Sun being in Libra or Taurus - Venus is Prime Significator.

The Sun being in Virgo or Gemini - Mercury is Prime Significator.

The Sun being in Leo - Sun is Prime Significator.

The Sun being in Cancer - Moon is Prime Significator.

When the Mon becomes P.S. through the Sun being in the sign Cancer, as happens from Midsummer Day onwards for a month, it is obvious that we cannot trace primary indications from the ephemeral aspects of so fast and variable a body as the Moon, so what is to be done? Experience says, Watch the position and aspect of the ASCENDING NODES of the Moon, which is given for the second and third day continuously throughout the year in any good ephemeris. <u>Merely trace [treat] the node as if it were the Moon itself and the rest follows in due sequence.</u>

A few tests of the early July charts will show how this works out. The NODE OF THE EARTH IS ALWAYS THE VERNAL EQUINOX, AND ALWAYS ZERO ARIES. BUT THE NODE OF THE MOON FROM WHICH ITS COURSE BEGINS, IS ONLY IN THE SAME LONGITUDE AFTER A PERIOD OF 19 YEARS. The node thus becomes a very important indicator. At the beginning of August 1914 it was in Pisces 7 and had no aspects. But it was then in the Decan of Saturn, and Saturn had a succession of bad aspects all through the first three weeks of that month, so that Cancerian Charts were under evil aspects at that time.

It will be observed that there is a line of sympathy between the New York and British Charts in that Venus is the common PRIME SIGNIFICATOR. In the New York Chart it is strong in its own sign Taurus and this perhaps accounts for the strong Hibernian affinity. In the British Chart (London) Venus is elevated in the sign Gemini, which is the ruling sign of the USA as a Republic. Consequently there is much sympathy of action between the two markets, and the coincidence of the midheaven degree is remarkable. It is not inappropriate either that the Moon in the NY Chart should be in the ruling sign of England, its P.S. in the ruling sign of Ireland, and Fortuna in the ruling sign of Scotland.

FORTUNA indicates the POSITION OF THE MOON AT THE TIME OF LOCAL SUNRISE FOR ANY SET DATE. IT IS MEASURED BY LONGITUDE, i.e., degrees and minutes of the zodiac.

THE COMPANY. In the case of a company, the M.C. is THE CHAIRMAN, THE 11TH HOUSE DENOTES THE DIRECTORS OR BOARD OF CONTROL, THE ASCENDANT DENOTES THE SHAREHOLDERS. THE SIXTH HOUSE SHOWS THE EMPLOYEES.

SPECIFIC HOUSE INDICATION.

THE FIRST HOUSE governs the PUBLIC in which is vested all forms of enterprise and development.

THE SECOND HOUSE relates to PRICE OF MONEY, TRADE, RETURNS, BULLION IMPORTS, BILLS OF EXCHANGE, etc.

THE THIRD HOUSE rules railroads, tramways, omnibuses, traction of all sorts, locomotion, telephone, aircraft, canals, bridges and transports as well as postal service and all means of communication.

THE FOURTH HOUSE rules real estate, land explorations, mines, developments, crops, produce of raw material from the soil.

THE FIFTH HOUSE shows educational matters, art, theatres, cinemas, amusements and schools.

THE SIXTH HOUSE governs foodstuffs, clothing equipment, outfitting supplies, upholstering, furnishings, building and upfitting.

THE SEVENTH HOUSE rules accountancy, banking, corporations, exchanges, contracts, equity, discounting, surveying, valuations, probate, etc.

THE EIGHTH HOUSE controls waste products, conservancy, dredging, petrol, parafine, benzine, medical accessories, chemicals and nitrates.

THE NINTH HOUSE is connected with insurance, cables, publishing, wireless, radiographs, liners and foreign affairs.

THE TENTH HOUSE rules state affairs, the government and political activity generally.

THE ELEVENTH HOUSE rules the Exchequer (treasury), bonds, government loans, electric and gaslight companies.

THE TWELFTH HOUSE rules laundries, breweries, fisheries, boot manufacturers, hosiery and GOLD STORAGE.

THE CHART OF THE HEAVENS FOR LONDON.

This is introduced in order to display the influence of ECLIPSES when falling on the places of the significators, either radical or progressed.

On the 12th of March 1914, there was an eclipse of the Moon which fell in Virgo 21. Incidentally, it happened to be in opposition to the ex-Kaiser's radical M.C. in Pisces 21. But what is more pertinent to our present study is the fact that Virgo 21 was the progressed M.C. for the London Exchange for the year 1914. Thus 59'8" daily mean motion of the Sun, multiplied by 113, the years elapsed since 1801, gives 111 deg. 26 min., or 3 signs, 21 degrees, 26 min. This being added to the M.C. of the radix, Taurus 28, gives Virgo 20 on the M.C. for 1914.

The Arcana, or Stock and Share Key

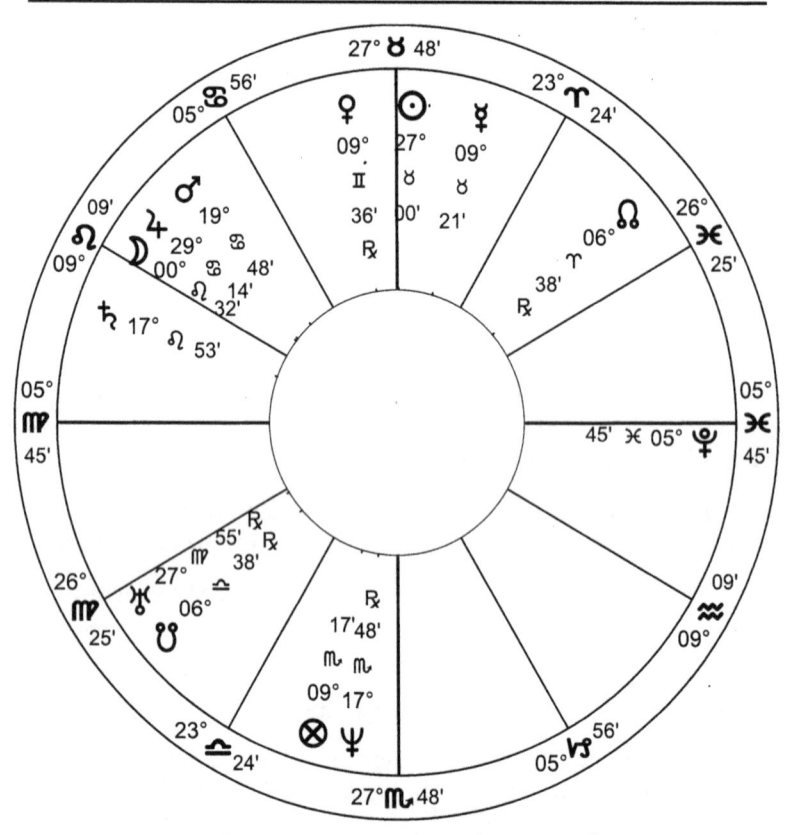

London Stock Exchange, May 18, 1801, noon LMT, London.
Placidus Houses, Mean Node.

Now Mars passed over the line of the eclipse in Virgo 20 on the 28-29th of July of that year and war was declared against Serbia by Austria on the 28th. On the 31st a state of war was declared in Germany, who declared war on Russia on the 31st or 1st of August and invaded Luxembourg on the same date, French territory being invaded on August 2nd. This war and the exact date of it was foreseen by "Sepharial" and notified by him in print throughout the country as early as July 1913.

Here we see how the meridian line of the Exchange horoscope, affecting all securities, was brought into line with the eclipse which immediately preceded the Great War, and how

The Arcana, or Stock and Share Key

both were brought into line with the meridian of the ex-Kaiser's horoscope. These considerations determined the prediction of War and the date was defined by the transit of Mars over the triple combine of Virgo Pisces meridian.

The fiscal troubles which have dominated all British politics arose from the eclipse of the meridian degree for the year 1914, and its effects could be traced right through to 1918, when, as early as August 1st, 1914, "Sepharial" fixed the end of the war in these words: "The war will be Titanic and will last until 1918 — The Hohenzollerns will bite the dust and gather the DEAD SEA fruit of an inordinate ambition."

When for the last time in the period of 4 years (duration of eclipse) Mars was in transit over the same point, Virgo 20, on March 21st, 1918, Germany launched its last great offensive. America was then well represented at the front and brought new blood into the conflict which was steadily wearing out the reserves of Germany. It was then said: "Hostilities will cease in November of this year." By adding the increment of mean motion for 4 years (1914-1918) to Virgo 20, we reach Virgo 24, and under this meridian in the latitude of London we find Scorpio 29:24 to be rising. This is in 60 degrees aspect to Jupiter, with a following 60 of the Moon in the radix, and this was followed by the 60 of the Sun to the place of Jupiter and the Moon. The ascendant at this time being past the opposition of the Sun and the trouble done and over, while Fortuna had come up to the sextile of the progressed M.C. at the opening of the WAR.

Fiscal troubles began to arise between America and Great Britain in 1928 on the question of War Debts, and had considerable influence on stock and share values. The total eclipse of May 19 fell on the meridian of the two charts. It will last until 1932, critical dates from the source being November 1929, July 1930 and October-November 1931.

Therefore we have reason to regard the action of eclipses as constituting a major influence upon the VALUE OF SECURITIES.

Better books make better astrologers. Here are some of our other titles:

AstroAmerica's Daily Ephemeris, 2000-2010
AstroAmerica's Daily Ephemeris, 2010-2020
AstroAmerica's Daily Ephemeris, 2000-2020
  - *all for Midnight. Compiled & formatted by David R. Roell*

Al Biruni
The Book of Instructions in the Elements of the Art of Astrology, *translated by R. Ramsay Wright*
  Western - Hindu blend with lots of Parts, from the great Persian sage

Derek Appleby
Horary Astrology: The Art of Astrological Divination
  The book by the man who revived horary astrology

C.E.O. Carter
An Encyclopaedia of Psychological Astrology
  A unique encyclopaedia of character & disease

Charubel & Sepharial
Degrees of the Zodiac Symbolized
  Two surprising sets, complete in one volume

H.L. Cornell, M.D.
Encyclopaedia of Medical Astrology
  958 pages, hardcover, the ultimate astro-medical reference

Nicholas Culpeper
Astrological Judgement of Diseases from the Decumbiture of the Sick, *and,* **Urinalia**
  Brief, intense, to the point.

Dorotheus of Sidon
Carmen Astrologicum, *translated by David Pingree*
  Masterful first century AD treatise of Greek astrology

Nicholas deVore
Encyclopedia of Astrology
  From 1948, the best modern reference

Firmicus Maternus
Ancient Astrology Theory & Practice: Matheseos Libri VIII, *translated by Jean Rhys Bram*
  After Ptolemy's Tetrabiblos, the most famous, the most studied astrology book

William Lilly
Christian Astrology, books 1 & 2
  The Introduction to Astrology, and the best horary book ever written
Christian Astrology, book 3
  One of the finest expositions of natal astrology. A surprise best-seller

Claudius Ptolemy
Tetrabiblos, *translated by J.M. Ashmand*
  The great book, in the classic translation.

Vivian Robson
Astrology and Sex
  One of the best guides to astrology & relationships
Electional Astrology
  Pick the best time for your new project
Fixed Stars & Constellations in Astrology
  The classic book, again in print

Richard Saunders
The Astrological Judgement and Practice of Physick
  By the Richard who inspired Ben Franklin's famous Almanac

Sepharial
Primary Directions, a definitive study
  A complete, detailed guide

James Wilson, Esq.
Dictionary of Astrology
  From 1820. Quirky, opinionated, a fascinating read

H.S. Green, Raphael & C.E.O. Carter
Mundane Astrology: *3 Books*
  Comprehensive guide to the mundane

If not available from your local bookseller, order directly from:
The Astrology Center of America
207 Victory Lane
Bel Air, MD 21014

on the web at:
http://www.astroamerica.com

Lightning Source UK Ltd.
Milton Keynes UK
UKHW010749130622
404345UK00001B/164